D1140764

THE WORLD'S EPOCH-MAKERS

EDITED BY
OLIPHANT SMEATON

Shirley Crutharie. 11/88.
(28)

Muhammad and
His Power

By P. De Lacy Johnstone, M.A.(Oxon.), M.R.A.S.

Muhammad and His Power

By

P. De Lacy Johnstone, M.A.(Oxon.), M.R.A.S.

(Of H.M.B.C.S., retired)

"The faith which he preached is compounded of an eternal truth and a necessary fiction : That there is only one God, and that Mahomet is the Prophet of God."

Gibbon.

Edinburgh. T. & T. Clark

1901

PRINTED BY
MORRISON AND GIBB LIMITED,

FOR

T. & T. CLARK, EDINBURGH.

LONDON: SIMPKIN, MARSHALL, HAMILTON, KENT, AND CO. LIMITED.
NEW YORK: CHARLES SCRIBNER'S SONS.

To

My Wife

PREFACE

So much has been written, and so much learning and study devoted to the history of Muhammad and the religious and political power which he founded, and which now, after thirteen centuries, seems—as a religion —not less firmly established than ever it was, that one who approaches the subject to-day cannot hope to do much more than sift and select from the labours of those who have gone before him. The struggle of Christianity with the forces of Islām began within five years of the Flight from Mecca, but the study of its documents and the history of its rise and progress (that is, of course, by those who are outside its pale) has been the growth of the last century and a half. In our own country the strength and, scarcely less, the weaknesses of the founder and of the system have roused the admiration of Gibbon and Carlyle, have been the object of profound study by such scholars and administrators as Edward Lane and Sir William Muir, and have been the goal of travellers like Richard Burton and Gifford Palgrave, Burkhardt and Carsten Niebuhr. In this, as in most other domains of knowledge, German scholars have done great work: the names of Sprenger and Weil, Nöldeke and Kremer, are specially to be honoured; while the great work of

Caussin de Perceval, and the masterly though short
book of St. Hilaire, are witness to the debt which we
owe in these studies to France also. To one book
I am myself under particular obligation—Hughes's
Dictionary of Islām, a work of great grasp and deep
learning, not only embodying the substance of the most
important work of his predecessors, but also instinct
with that familiarity with his theme which can only
be got by a life spent among Muhammadans, together
with wide study of their literature and modes of
thought. Having thus made a general acknowledgment
of the sources of the present work, it will not be
necessary to burden my pages with particular refer-
ences, and the reader will readily excuse me from
making them. One part of the field of inquiry still lies
imperfectly worked, the relation of Islām to Judaism,
which was made a reproach to Muhammad by his
unbelieving countrymen: it is to be hoped that some
day we shall have exhaustive treatment of the subject,
on the lines already drawn by those brilliant Jewish
scholars, Deutsch and Geiger. The earlier chapters of
the book give a sketch of the land, the people, and the
conditions in which the Prophet arose, for he was an
Arab of the Arabs; in the latest is shown how his
successors prosecuted his work, and some account is
given of that wonderful Qurān which is the Charter
of Islām.

The following short list of books, easily accessible
in our own language, will give the student sound
knowledge of my whole subject, and will guide him to
the best original authorities, if he desire to consult
them :—

Sir W. Muir's *Life of Mahomet* and *Early Caliphate*

(Smith & Elder); Hughes, *Dictionary of Islām* (Allen); Sell's *Faith of Islām* (Trübner); Lane's *Selections from the Kurān* (Trübner) and *Modern Egyptians* (Murray); Burton's *Pilgrimage to Al-Medina and Meccah* (Tylston & Edwards), and W. G. Palgrave's *Central and Eastern Arabia* (Macmillan); Koelle's *Muhammad and Muhammadanism* (Longmans); Palmer's *Qurān* (Clarendon Press) and Sale's *Koran*, the latter of which is still in many respects unsurpassed. The *Encyclopædia Britannica* articles ARABIA (Palgrave), and MUHAMMAD, etc. (Nöldeke), are also very valuable.

The portrait of Muhammad, gathered from the Traditions (p. 148), is taken almost exactly from Deutsch's *Essay on Islām*: Mr. Poole had already used it before me.

The passages from the *Qurān* are taken, by permission of the Delegates of the Clarendon Press, from Professor Palmer's version. I am also greatly indebted to Sir C. J. Lyall for leave to make extracts from his *Ancient Arabian Poetry* (pp. 20–24).

ON THE TRANSLITERATION OF
ARABIC WORDS

———+———

THERE exists unhappily great diversity among scholars in the transcribing of Arabic words in Roman characters, and the difficulties are made greater by differences of pronunciation (both of vowels and consonants) in the various countries where Arabic is spoken. I therefore ask the indulgence of readers for faults and inconsistencies of spelling: scholars will not be severe, and I might shelter myself behind the authority and example of one of our greatest Arabists, Sir R. Burton, who pronounced all special efforts after scientific accuracy to be "superfluous for the reader who knows Arabic, and no help to the reader who does not." My own rough scheme is meant only as a guide to correct pronunciation.

That vowels are to be pronounced as in Italian is the general rule, consonants as in English; long vowels are marked with a bar, but where the pronunciation has once been correctly indicated, it may be found that sometimes such marks have been omitted when a name recurs.

a—the so-called obscure vowel—as *u* in m*u*d
ā   „ *a* „ f*a*ther
i   „ *i* „ b*i*t
ī   „ *ee* „ m*ee*t
u   „ *oo* „ f*oo*t
ū   „ *oo* „ f*oo*d
e   „ *ay* „ p*ay*
ai   „ *ai* „ *ai*sle
au   „ *ow* „ *ow*l
th   hard as in *th*ought
dh   soft as in fa*th*er
Kh   Greek χ as in Sc. lo*ch*
q   represents guttural *K*
gh is a strong guttural (ghain), not very different from the French *r*.

Ain, the peculiar Semitic guttural, I have generally left unrepresented; but sometimes, as in the common name *Saad*, and in *Kaaba*, it is represented by the second vowel. Generally, where two vowels (not being one of the diphthongs *ai*, *au*) come together, both are to be pronounced.

After much hesitation I have uniformly written the Prophet's name Muhammad, though most English readers will probably always follow the traditional pronunciation Mahomet. In the case of the Khalifa I have used the familiar *Omar* instead of the correct *Umr*, the latter being hard to pronounce and the former particularly familiar as the name also of the Persian poet Omar Khayyām. *Khalifa* replaces the old title *Caliph*, and is only too well known to English readers from recent events in the Soudan. Mecca and Medīna are written in the traditional way.

In proper names I have written *al* (the definite article), not changing *l* before dentals, etc., as is done in pronunciation.

SOME LEADING DATES IN THE HISTORY

A.D.

570. Attack by Abraha on Mecca repulsed. "Year of the Elephant." MUHAMMAD born.
595. Marriage to Khadīja.
611. Muhammad declares himself the Apostle of God
615–616. First and Second Migration of Converts to Abyssinia.
617. Muslims placed under a ban at Mecca.
620. Death of Khadīja and of Abu Tālib.
621. First Pledge of Aqaba.
622. The Hijra. Flight of Muhammad to Medīna.
624. Battle of Badr.
630. Capture of Mecca.
632. Death of Muhammad.
632 to 634. Abu Bakr Khalifa. Subjugation of Arabia. First foreign conquests.
634. Omar Khalifa.
634. First Recension of the Qurān.
634. Victory of Yarmūk.
635. Victory at Qadīsiya.
637. Conquest of Jerusalem.
641. Conquest of Egypt.
642. Conquest of Persia.
644. Murder of Omar. Election of Uthmān.
651. Revision of the Qurān : text finally settled.
656. Murder of Uthmān : election of Ali. Battle of the "Camel."

A.D.

657. Battle of Siffīn, against Muāwiya.
658. Ali deposed by the Umpires.
661. Murder of Ali.   Hasan abdicates : Muāwiya sole Khalifa.
680. Husain defeated and slain at Karbalā.

CONTENTS

b   xv

CONTENTS

CHAPTER X

CHAPTER XI

CHAPTER XII

CHAPTER XIII

CHAPTER XIV

CHAPTER XV

APPENDICES

MUHAMMAD AND HIS POWER

———◆———

CHAPTER I

The Awakening of Arabia—Early Commerce—Mecca and
Muhammad—His Mission and the Extension of his Power
—Physical Features and Ethnology—The Hijāz—Bedouins.

ARABIA, which had slept for ages, isolated by difference of climate and of race, was at last to awake; her
warring tribes were to be knit together in one faith,
and in obedience to one master-mind; the mists of her
hoary idolatries were to roll away before the sun of a
new doctrine, and the veil behind which the constituents
of the new nation had been for centuries hid from the
peoples around, was once and for all to be rent asunder.
The sixth century after Christ was nearing its close;
Christianity itself was, alas! torn by bitter strife and
faction; the mighty empire of Rome, whose seat had
been three centuries before changed from the banks of
Tiber to the shores of the Bosphorus, was sinking into
decrepitude; the rival empire of Persia also had lost
the vigour of earlier times; the world was ripe for the
appearance of a fresh race; and in the fulness of time
the Prophet of Arabia was born in Mecca, which had

long been, as history witnesses, a centre of religion and
of commerce, from which radiated ideas and traffic to
every corner of the great peninsula, and to all the lands
whither her merchants travelled. It was but a small
town, nestling in a plain amid arid, volcanic rocks,
some 50 miles from the shores of the Red Sea, from
which the ground rises gradually toward the great tableland of inner Arabia; but to it, as to a sanctuary of
great holiness, to worship at the rude temple which
legend traced back to Abraham and Ishmael as its
founders, gathered, year by year in their thousands, the
merchants and poets, travellers and traders, of every
tribe and nation of Arabia. As the rival peoples of
Greece mingled on the plains of Olympus or Corinth,
or the merchants of many lands meet to-day at the
great fair of Nijni-Novgorod, or as pilgrims flock to
Rome from all corners of the habitable earth,—so in
pagan times, in the days of the "Ignorance," did the
wandering desert tribes gather for pleasure, for profit,
and for worship, to the plains around Mecca. They
worshipped the three hundred and sixty idols that
stood round the Kaaba; they made the mystic sevenfold circuit of the shrine, and they drank of the holy
well Zemzem; and, above all, they devoutly kissed
the wondrous Black Stone, that holiest part of the Holy
Temple's walls. These bonds of union, purified from
idolatrous taint, were retained and strengthened in the
new religion; and the most notable duty of Islām, the
annual pilgrimage to Mecca, a sacred obligation laid on
every follower of the Prophet, to be discharged once at
least in his lifetime, if it be in any wise possible, has
its roots deep in the immemorial usages of pagan
Arabia.

In the year 570 of the Christian era, probably on the 20th of August, was born to his widowed mother Amīna, Muhammad ("the Praised"), grandson and ward of the aged Abd al Muttalib, the venerable chief of Mecca, who rejoiced greatly over his birth; for Abdallah, the child's father, lately dead, was best-beloved of his many sons. The fond imagination of later times wove around the child's birth, and his parents and ancestry for many generations, tales of wonder on which we need not linger: a light of glory had passed from one patriarch to another, marking out the blessed line in which the last of the Prophets was to be born; his mother (as her time drew near) was visited by wondrous dreams, foreshadowing the matchless grandeur that awaited her child; and in distant Persia, so runs the legend, the throne and city of the great King-of-Kings were shaken by a mighty earthquake. The child was indeed born to such a marvellous destiny, his achievements in the sixty-three years of his allotted span of life were so great, his influence on all after-ages has been so profound and widespread, the personal devotion of hundreds of millions of men, who have in the past thirteen centuries looked on him as all but divine, so intense, that no wonders of legend can surprise us, and we note them as evidence of the deep veneration which the highest human power will always command from men. Yet, as his followers call their religion— after his own example—not by the Teacher's name, but Islām, "self-surrender" (to God Almighty), so do they reckon their Era, as we shall hereafter see, not from his birth, but from the turning-point of his life, the Hijra ("Hegira") or Flight from Mecca to Medīna, when at the age of fifty-two he ceased to be merely the Preacher to a

gainsaying people, a " Warner " with no commission or
authority to compel, and became, at the head of a small
band of devoted followers, ever-increasing thenceforward,
a temporal Chief as well as a Prophet of righteousness,
able and resolved to force on all the tribes of Arabia belief
in One God and in himself as the chosen Apostle of God.

The expansion of Muhammad's views we shall trace
in his life, together with the development of his
character. Like Buddhism and Christianity, Islām is
a missionary religion, as every living faith must be;
but the ways by which each of the three religions
has extended its dominion have differed widely, and
we are entitled to judge the spirit of each not only
by its methods, but by the commands of the founder
on the matter. Of Buddhism we know too little to
say whether force and authority were used to extend
it, but assuredly the gentle Gautama never sanctioned
such a course, and the four hundred millions of
Buddhists may be claimed as nations subdued by
peaceful means; in regard to our own Christian faith,
we must sadly admit that it has been too often
advanced by the sword, and by every engine of civil
and temporal compulsion, but this has been done in
direct defiance of the Master's commands, whether
given by Himself or by His disciples; but the spirit of
Islām is the opposite, and the Prophet, who two years
before his end had forbidden all but his own followers
to approach the hallowed shrines of Mecca, left on his
deathbed the solemn command that only Islām should
be tolerated in the confines of Arabia. Outside the
peninsula the command was less absolute: the choice
was to be offered of Islām or tribute, but submission to
one or the other alternative was required. The Suc-

cessors of the Prophet carried out his commands only too well, and their fierce and gallant soldiery, before whose earnest faith were set the joys of Paradise to every man who fell in battle for the religion, went forth conquering and to conquer, east and west, and north and south, till the banners of Islām floated from the Pillars of Hercules to the shores of the Yellow Sea. The tide has ebbed in some directions, but in others it has flowed. The Iberian peninsula has shaken off the chains of Islām, though it has replaced them by others; in Eastern Europe the tide was stayed more than two hundred years ago by John Sobieski before the walls of Vienna; but elsewhere the progress of Mahomet-anism, in one form or another, more simple or more complex, has been steady and sure. Among the millions of India its conquests are considerable; in Africa—though there it is so closely allied to the cruel and accursed system of slavery—it is making much headway; while the maritime provinces of China form its most eastern bulwark. In his lifetime the Prophet foretold that his followers would be split up into no less than seventy-three sects—he credited the Christian with seventy-two!—of which one only would hold the true faith; and the prediction might be justified by historical evidence; but heresy and schism seem to do little to weaken the aggressive force of the religion, and to-day, though politically far less powerful than of old, one-sixth of the whole human race own its sway, and are ready to fight or to endure to face death and to inflict it, with the battle-cry: "There is no god but the God, and Muhammad is the Prophet of God!"

It is a commonplace to speak of the influence of

climate and geographical conditions upon the nature
and thought of the inhabitants of a land, and the
physical character of the Arabian peninsula is so
singular that we may readily believe that it has had
special power to mould the mind and manners of its
peoples. As the dreamy vagueness and philosophic
despair of Buddhism [1] sprang up in the congenial soil of
the hot, moist valley of the Ganges, so did the fiery,
arid lands of Arabia, diversified with barren, volcanic
ranges of hills, swept by sand-laden whirlwinds, and
offering to its hardy indwellers few and far-separated
oases, give birth to the stern warrior-faith of Islām.
Arabia, divided from the African continent by the
Red Sea and from the rest of Asia by the Persian
Gulf on the east and the Syrian desert on the north,
stretches southward to the Indian Ocean in the shape
of an axe-head, between the parallels of 31° and
13° N. lat., and those of 34° and 60° E. long., of
which at least two-thirds is an uninhabitable desert,
and where the settled states are divided from one
another by great stretches of sand. The Arabian
peninsula extends over an area of nearly a million and
a quarter square miles, about four-fifths of India or
China proper. Yet its population is calculated by
Palgrave (1864) as no more than seven or eight millions,
of whom he reckons about one-seventh only as nomad.
In Muhammad's days it was no doubt greater. The
country that extends along the southern shores of the
Persian Gulf and the Sea of Omān, facing Persia across
the sea, and for ages forming part of the Persian Empire,

[1] Indian Buddhism, the early doctrine. The florid, degenerate forms
that prevail in Burma, in China, in Tibet, and in Mongolia have little
save the name to connect them with the teaching of Gautama.

as it enjoys a good climate, and is well watered, so it has always been a highly favoured land, a land of wealth and settled habitation. When one passes away from the coast-lands, crossing the western barrier of hills, the great pathless sandy desert stretches in front of the traveller for 12 or 14 degrees of latitude before he reaches the barren, broken mountain-chain which stretches at various distances nearly parallel to the coast of the Red Sea. The northern part of this chain is known specially as the Hijaz or Boundary-land, and there—in a plain among the arid, volcanic hills—lies Mecca, the birthplace of Muhammad, and scene of his earlier preaching, whilst Medīna, the cradle of his kingdom and his last resting-place, lies about 240 miles due north, and at a distance from the sea at Yambu much greater than that of Mecca from its seaport at Jedda. This is the sacred land of Islām, the blessed country of the "Two Sanctuaries" (Haramain), whither flock, in long lines, year by year at the sacred season, converging streams of pilgrims from the remotest corners of Asia and Africa, to fulfil the great duty of pilgrimage, laid upon the conscience of every pious Muslim, to be performed (if health and circumstances do not absolutely prevent) once in his lifetime. In this, too, Islām has borrowed from the kindred nation of Israel, and the followers of Muhammad traverse the hills that stand round about Mecca or Medīna to gather in the hallowed plains, as the Israelites of old flocked to Jerusalem at the great Passover Feast. Then, too, during the sacred months, a truce of God is proclaimed, though in these degenerate times the robber tribes of the desert and the fanatical Wahhābis make little scruple of attacking and plundering the pilgrim caravans, whether they come from the orthodox centres of Stamboul, Cairo, and Bombay, or from the heretical land of Persia.

The Hijāz, then, the sacred land of Islām, from which the new religion went forth to conquer first the great Arabian peninsula, and then a large part of the decaying Roman Empire, and to sweep eastwards in its triumphant march to the shores of the China Sea, is a country lying between the mountain-chain that divides it from the vast central tableland of Arabia and the Red Sea. It is an irregular parallelogram of about 250 miles in length by 150 in breadth, and the barren, sandy soil affords but scanty subsistence to its inhabitants. From of old caravans had held their way through, southward from Egypt and Palestine, northward from Hadramaut and the shores of the Indian Ocean, and a very recent traveller, Mr. Bent, followed with interest the now deserted paths worn by countless thousands of camels in the far-off centuries when transit by sea was rare and timid. Those southern lands of Arabia seem, though trustworthy record there is none, to be the home of the earliest races of the peninsula, pushed down before invaders of a higher type. To the north stretches a pathless desert of sand, roughly from 15° to 24° N. lat., and from 45° to 56° E. long.; to the west and south lies Yaman, Arabia "the Happy" (more properly "of the right hand"); further north the more fertile, settled, and powerful kingdom of Najd, the seat now of Wahhābi power, the *caput mortuum* of puritan Islām, whose dry tableland, bounded on every side by wide belts of desert, is the home of the noblest breed of Arab horses. Beyond the desert belt to the north-west is the Shammar highland state, then more desert, and then at length the fertile tracts of Syria and Mesopotamia, scene of the first foreign conquests of Islām. The above very brief sketch of the Arabian peninsula and its chief divisions will explain its isolation, and how it defied through the ages all attempts to conquer or even to explore it. Roman poets might tell of its fabled riches, and Jewish myth might vaunt its marvels, but the legions of Rome won but few and fleeting victories on its soil, and retired vanquished, or left their bones to whiten on its pathless deserts and under its pitiless sun.

From the land we pass to the people. The evidence of language shows conclusively that the peninsula has been peopled, apart from a trifling admixture of African blood, by a Semitic race, kindred to Hebrews, Phœnicians, and Assyrians; but the permanence of language-type is so great as to leave a profound scholar like Wright in doubt which of the sister-tongues, Assyrian or Arabic, was the elder. Arabian historians before Muhammad there were none, and those who came after joined to the want of critical method minds warped by theologic bias. The pious Muslim was bound to trace the origin of the nation back through Ishmael to Abraham, and then back to our first father Adam, who himself built the sacred Kaaba ("Cube-house") after the model of the heavenly temple which had been shown him in a vision. Palgrave inclines to think that the lowest stratum of the Arab peoples came eastward from Africa, and that the northern invasion was also of African origin, modified by previous settlement in Asia, and driven south before the Turanian wave. This, however, in the face of the evidence from language, does not seem a safe view; the settlement indicated in Genesis, adopted and enlarged by Arabic tradition, and systematised in the Qurān and the Traditions of the Prophet, which ascribes the final peopling of North Arabia to about 2000 B.C., is certainly nearer the truth.

As far back as we have any record, the inhabitants have been divided into the nomad Bedouins (Bidāwi = man of the desert) and the folk of the town. The former led, and to this day lead, an unsettled life, driving their flocks and herds from pasture to pasture divided into small tribal groups, loosely compacted in larger clans. Passionate, cunning, and revengeful, they carry on the blood-feud from generation to generation; their much-praised loyalty to their salt may be gauged by the undoubted fact that frequently they have led hapless travellers and whole caravans astray in the desert, there to perish from thirst, that their faithless guides might serve themselves heirs to their property; and the fervour of their religion is shown by their own saying, quoted by Burton: "We pray not, because we must drink the water of ablution; we give no alms, because we ask them (sturdy beggars they are too!); we fast not the Ramazan month, because we starve throughout the year; and we do no pilgrimage, because the world is the House of Allah." Till Muhammad welded them for a time into a warrior nation they had owned no common bond of union, and the bands were soon again relaxed after the work of conquest, even as the tribes have for the most part thrown off the garb of his religion and fallen back into their primitive paganism. Sun-worship is widely prevalent, their ideas of a future life are crude and vague, and gross superstition darkens their lives. Their slender wealth

consists in horses for battle or the chase, in herds of
camels, flocks of sheep and goats, and the few black
tents that form their encampments. The tribal government is scarcely effective, and "every man does that
which is right in his own eyes," so long as he does not
incur the dread penalty of the blood-feud. Naturally,
each tribe has its own recognised area to wander over,
and encroachment is jealously resisted; and any tribe
that is wronged in its honour or its possessions can
reckon to the uttermost on support from all those with
which it counts kindred or alliance.

Tho men of tho towns, on the other hand, following
the peaceful ways of commerce, sending out their caravans, and having multiplied relations with foreign lands
and peoples; delighting in social intercourse, so far as
the jealous seclusion of women is compatible therewith,
—these have attained to a plane of civilisation far above
the desert-rangers. The latter, the "men of the tent,"
heartily despise the townsmen, the "men of the walls,"
levy tribute on them for safe passage of themselves
and their goods, and let slip no chance of pillaging
them when they can do so in safety. The desert Arab,
brave to desperation when necessary, has no wish to
risk life or limb when he can avoid it. He feels no
shame in methods of attack or defence that more
civilised nations brand as cowardly or even treacherous,
for usually his object is plunder only, and on the life of
others he sets no high price, though he be very careful
of his own,—and of that of anyone whom he holds to
be under his guard or protection. The old chivalrous
feelings, which in the golden days of the "Ignorance"
bound the host to do all things for the safety, honour,
and welfare of his guest, still hold sway in the desert;

the tie of "brotherhood," usually formed by the Eastern means of a present, secures the stranger from wrong, though it is highly dangerous to presume very far on the immunity, and those who have travelled among the tribes strongly advise all who follow their example not to make any display that might excite the covetousness of their hosts.[1] The picture which the evidence compels one to draw of the social and moral state and qualities which really prevail in Arabia is not attractive, nor is it that with which our fancy is familiar. In the next chapter we shall see the more pleasing image which is presented by the poets and annalists to whom we are indebted for all we know of Arab ways and thoughts in the days before Muhammad,—the "times of Ignorance," as Muslims count all the ages before his revelation opened the eyes of their mind to the duties of life and the awful realities of the afterworld.

[1] This is from Burton's *Pilgrimage*.   Elsewhere he says : "The baser sort of Badawi is never to be trusted : he is a traitor born.   Neither oath nor kindness can bind him : he unites the cruelty of the cat with the wildness of the wolf."   Palgrave says much the same.

CHAPTER II

The Arabs before Islām—Social Condition—Religious Beliefs—
Arab Poetry and Arab Life—Tribal Ties—Hātim Tai—
Select Specimens of pre-Islāmic Poetry.

An eloquent scholar in our own day laments that we
can no longer see the true Arab as he was in the
"time of the Ignorance,"—"a noble type of man,
though there be nobler." Muhammad, he adds, in part
destroyed the Arab in creating the Muslim, and
effected thereby a temporary good and a lasting
harm. There is ground for Mr. Poole's lament, but it
is the law of this world that no advance can be made
without the sacrifice of something that we would not
willingly miss, and it is easy to be carried away by
enthusiasm for the past, when its beauties have been
embalmed in deathless poems, while its darker features
have been softened or altogether obliterated by the
merciful fingers of time. With men and with nations
the same principle holds, that we speak "good only of
the dead"; as the splendid valour and constancy and
skill of Cæsar blaze in our histories, and his ruthless
massacres and enslavement of whole nations in Gaul
are forgotten; as in almost our own day the brilliant
strategy and victories of the first Napoleon have
drawn a veil of glamour over his crooked policy, his
treacheries, his mercilessness,—even so have the poets

13

of Arabia thrown a halo of glory round the lives and
deeds of the old heroes of the wild. The picture
drawn by the converts to Islām of the state in which
they and their forefathers had lived, "without God
and without hope in the world," till Muhammad
brought his revelation, is a very dark one, as we shall
see hereafter; and it is necessary to bear in mind their
witness while we listen to the more pleasing music
of old Arab "criticism of life." New converts would,
in their fervid zeal for the faith they had embraced,
inevitably deepen the shadows in the picture they
drew of the life they had forsaken, but the old poets
would as certainly heighten its beauties and disguise
its loathly characters. The legislation of the new
religion proves an earlier state of morals and manners
terrible in the extreme; questions recorded in the
Traditions reveal the common practice of wickedness
to which one dare not allude; the absolute instability
of the marriage tie, the great prevalence of female
infanticide; and the hard measure commonly dealt
out to orphans, are but a few of the darker traits
that marked the life of the older desert polity. For
this last misery Muhammad, himself born after his
father's death, and in early childhood bereaved of a
well-loved mother also, was peculiarly sympathetic and
pitiful; and no part of his law excites our admiration
more than that in which he preaches justice, kindness,
loving care for those whom fate has bereft of their
natural guardians, and with burning eloquence lays
down the high duty of filial love and obedience.[1]

[1] A tradition tells that he ordered one of his followers to put away
the wife he loved because his father desired it. Again he said, "The
keys of Paradise lie at a mother's feet."

All who have travelled in the desert are agreed in the matchless charm of its clear, life-giving air. It casts a spell over body and mind which is vainly sought elsewhere, and he who has once known the witchery of the secret of the desert, with its sense of unfettered freedom amid infinite solitudes, thinks of it ever after with unspeakable joy and regret. If such be the feelings of Western travellers, who in their desert wanderings must miss all the softness and comfort of their common daily existence, we shall not wonder at the intensity of life that coursed in the veins of the children of the wild. Men of strong passions were they, fiery of temper, ardent in love and bitter in hate; delighting in war, in the chase, and the banquet; not sparing of the wine-cup at the feast, but of unmatched tolerance of cold and thirst and hunger when need was. If they did not "lisp in numbers," the natural harmonies of their tongue lent grace, dignity, and eloquence to their utterance; they delighted in every form of poetry and eloquence, praise of themselves, their kindred, and their friends, or bitter shafts of blame and satire against their foes; and the wonderful instrument which Muhammad wielded to crush his enemies, to inspire his followers, to preach the Faith, or to curse the foes thereof,—in the one great "miracle" of which he boasted, his Qurān,—was forged and perfected under the black tents of the Bedouins, where its echoes may still be caught in almost unsullied purity. The Prophet himself frowned upon poetry and poets, though he confessed their power, and was glad to use the weapon of satire against his enemies,—though, alas! nearly all the chief poets of his time were

arrayed against him; to music also he was strangely
dull, which is the more to be wondered at as his
nervous susceptibility was great, and the powerful,
deep tones of his staunch Bilāl—who first called the
Faithful to public prayer, and who held his high office
for twenty long years — was more grateful to the
Prophet's heart than sweetest strains of harp or pipe.[1]

But when the stern strain of the earlier struggles
and triumphs of the Faith were overpast, when
Muhammad and the grave Companions had gone to
their rest, when pomp and luxury had revived in
the new capitals of Damascus and Baghdad, then was
the old speech and poetry of the desert diligently
sought out and recorded.   Learned men strove to
steep themselves in the old fountains of eloquence,
the springs of which were fast drying up, and the
priceless treasures of poetry were gathered—known
to us as the *Muallaqāt*[2] or Seven Odes, the fairest
gems in Arabia's crown of poesy; the *Hamāsa* or
Heroic Lays, a collection of lyric gems, grave and gay,
trumpet-calls to battle, praise of the mighty dead,
love-songs and dirges and satires—a priceless and
unique mirror of old Arab life; and the Book of
Songs (*Kitāb al Aghānī*), where music is wedded to
the verse, if haply the old spirit could be recalled,
and the echoes of the old melodies be revived.   These
are the chief treasure-houses of old Arab poetry, but
there are also collections of tribal poems and the
works of single authors (as of Imr ul Kais and Labīd),

---

[1] Poetic feeling is not seldom divorced from love of music.   In our
own time, Mr. Swinburne is said to be strangely dead to music, whilst
Robert Browning was a great lover of it.

[2] Not the "Suspended" Poems, as used to be said : they never were
hung up in the Kaaba, nor were they written in letters of gold.

which have been the delight of generation after generation,—monuments more enduring than brass of the great warrior poets and *poetesses* that lived and loved, and fought and sang in the days of the "Ignorance."

The Arab of the desert then, as we find him in his poets, was brave, generous, hospitable, and loyal of heart. No sacrifice was too great, nor any danger too terrible, for him to meet in the cause of his family, his tribe, or his guest. Love for friend, or wife, or child; pride in his own valour and exploits, and in the glory of his clan and its connections; laments for the worthy dead, and passionate cries for vengeance, or savage delight in wreaking it; strange weird pictures of dimly-guessed existence beyond the grave, when the storms and the hopes and the joys and the troubles of life are past,—all these we find in the old Arab poetry. There too we find the lover's longings and the bridegroom's gladness, frank, trustful society of young men and maidens, the complete confidence of the warrior-chief in the wife who bore his children, who rules his household wisely and nobly, in whom his heart trusts, and who "shall do him good and not evil all the days of his life." The condition of women at all events, the true measure of all civilisation, could scarcely have been higher than it was among the Arabs of the desert; how that condition was lowered, and the character and self-respect of half the race degraded by Islām, will be told in its place. Writing, of course, there was little or none, the literature of the desert was preserved "living on the lips of men" and graven on the tablets of their hearts; the perfect warrior was also a famous poet, and the

2

name of many a poetess adorns the Arab bead-roll of
glory. The staple of their poetry is, however, largely
a description of the joys of battle, the struggle for
mastery, and the perils of the long, dark journeyings
through the waste; the noble horse and camel, the
keen, flashing sword in the battle, the deadly lance
and arrow; the swift, sudden storms that sweep over
mountain and plain, driving the goats and wild
antelopes in panic fear to their fastnesses, while the
lightning flashes, and the thunder roars, and the rain-
torrents hurry down the stony watercourses,—these
are the themes of their song. And prefaced to nearly
every one of the longer poems is a wail of lament
over the ashes of a long-deserted encampment, once
the home of a beloved maiden, a tearful note of human
sorrow to attune the heart to softened melancholy.
One type, one theme, is strangely absent from it all,—
the devotional. Praise or prayer is seldom heard,
though wild and terrible oaths are not wanting. The
old Arab was above all things self-centred, self-reliant,
confident that the cunning of his own strong right
hand could conquer fate. His worship did not greatly
pervade his life or his thoughts, and the shadowy
terrors with which he peopled the waste,—jinns and
ghūls and ghostly owls that wailed around the graves,
thirsting for the blood of requital, were rather gloomy
phantoms than real terrors. The warrior would take
the arrows of divination, but if the answer squared
not with his desire, he would hurl them back wrath-
fully and scornfully in the face of his idol.

Family or perhaps, rather, tribal pride was one of
the strongest passions among the Arabs. Every man
among them was a skilled genealogist, and no member

of an inferior clan was admitted to mate with a maiden
of more exalted degree. This it was that, as among the
proud Rajput races in India, prompted the murder of
infant daughters. But, within the limits which family
honour laid down, an Arab maiden was pretty free to
choose her own husband. Very often, however, it was
made a condition of marriage that the husband should
join his wife's clan; the children followed the mother's
kindred, and the wife was as free to dismiss her
husband for good cause—and such was liberally con-
strued—as the husband to put away his wife. Dis-
missal was commonly signified by no more formality
than turning about the door of the tent. One notable
historical instance is the divorce of the noble Hātim,
whose name is for ever famous for unstinted liberality.
Brave, loyal, generous, it is told of him that, when
almost starving along with his family, he slew his
peerless warhorse to make a feast for the hungry family
of a poor neighbour who appealed to him. Again,
when he had smitten down in battle a mortal foe and
held him at his mercy, he yielded up his own spear and
presented himself defenceless, " because he asked a gift
of me." Even as a boy, when tending his grandfather's
camels, he slew of them one apiece to feast three
wandering poets from Hīra, and presented them each
with one hundred in return for poems in praise of
himself and his tribe. It is not easy to condemn the
wife who, for her children's sake, put away such a
wasteful lord, nor does it seem just to condemn her
(as Mr. Poole does) for niggardliness. The story of
Hātim's divorce has its chief value in showing the
complete power which even the married women retained
over themselves. Many recent scholars have pushed

the inference much further, and have maintained that
down even to late pre-Islāmic times kindred was
counted in Arabia, as it is to this day in many barbarous parts of the world, through the mothers, and not
in the male line. The evidence does not seem to
warrant the conclusion, but the whole subject is worthy
of study; the retention of the children as part of the
mother's clan is natural enough in a state of society
where power depended on the numbers that could
stand up to "speak with their enemies in the gate,"
where the individual family was merged in the clan;
and the principle finds its parallel in the pretensions
at the present day of the Church of Rome in mixed
marriages. It may be added that the bond of blood
was peculiarly strong, and a young clansman had by
general tribal law the first claim on the hand of his
cousin, so much so that "daughter of my uncle" was
almost synonymous with " wife."

To the prose of my picture I now add as a pendant,
some few passages chosen from Sir C. J. Lyall's *Ancient
Arabian Poetry*, than which not many books are more
delightful to a lover of poetry, or more instructive and
stimulating to a scholar.

First we have two or three snatches of song,
showing the delights of peaceful life, and how the
Arab looked forward to Death, the "abridger of
delights and separator of friends." Both in their
gladder and their sadder strains they match well
with Horace.

> " Roast flesh, the glow of fiery wine,
>   to speed on camel fleet and sure,
> As thy soul lists to urge her on
>   through all the hollow's breadth and length;

White women, statue-like, that trail
  rich robes of price with golden hem,
Wealth, easy lot, no dread of ill,
  to hear the lute's complaining string,—

These are Life's joys. For man is set
  the prey of Time, and Time is change.
Life strait or large, great store or nought,
  all's one to Time, all men to Death."

And so the poet goes on to name men and races of old
renown whom Time and Death had swept away, in
tones that remind us of the lingering laments of
Horace or Villon.

"CARPE DIEM!"

" Come, friend and fellow, come—for sometimes is Folly sweet !
  so come, let us greet our band of drinkers aglow with wine,
And wash from our hearts sour speech of wisdom with cups
    abrim,
    and cut short the Ills of Life with laughter and jest and
    joy !

Yea, when once a moment comes of rest from the whirl, be
    quick
  and grasp it : for Time's tooth bites and quits not ; and
    mischief waits ;
And sure, if a bright hour lifts thy soul to a little peace,
  enough in thy path there lies of shadow and grief and
    pain."

"EHEU, FUGACES"

" Alas, my soul, for Youth that's gone—
  no light thing lost I when he fled !

What time I trailed my skirts in pride
  and shook my locks at the tavern's door.

Nay, envy not a man that men
  say, ' Age has made him ripe and wise' :

Though thou love life and live long safe,
  long living leaves its print on thee ! "

"THE PLACE THAT KNEW THEM KNOWS THEM NO MORE."

"Before the door of each and all a slumber-place is ready set
    men wane and dwindle, and the graves in number grow
    from day to day :

And ever more and more outworn the traces fade of hearth
    and home,
        and over yonder for some dead is newly built a house of
        clay.

Yea, neighbours are they of the living : near and close their
    fellowship ;
        but if thy soul would seek their converse, thou must seek
        it far away."

From the contemplation of death we rise to thoughts of
the Almighty, All-wise Ruler, who rewards every man
according to his works, a thought anterior to Islām,
and probably borrowed from Jewish or Christian
teaching—

"Yea, the righteous shall keep the way of the righteous,
    and to God turn the steps of all that abideth ;

And to God ye return, ye too ; with Him only
    rest the issues of things and all that they gather.

All that is in His Book of Knowledge is reckoned,
    and before Him revealed lies all that is hidden.

It boots not to hide from God aught evil within your hearts :
    it will not be hid—what men would hold back from God,
    He knows.

It may be its meed comes late : in the Book is the wrong set
    down
        for the Reckoning Day : it may be that vengeance is swift
        and stern."

Now follows part of the dirge which a brave chief
sang for himself when, before his death, he faced the
foes that had overwhelmed him—

" Upbraid me not, ye twain : enough is the shame for me
    to be as I am : no gain upbraiding to you or me.

Know ye not that in reproach is little that profits men ?
    it was not my wont to blame my brother when I was free.

.   .   .   .

Mulaika, my wife, knows well that time was when I stood
    forth
    a lion to lead men on or face those that rushed on me.

Yea, many the slaughtered beast I gave to the gamers, oft
    I journeyed alone where none would venture to share my
    way ;

And ofttimes I slew, to feast my fellows, the beast I rode,
    and ofttimes I rent my robe in twain for two singing-girls.

And when 'neath the stress of spears our steeds plunged and
    broke and backed,
    yea, mine were the fingers deft that turned from our line
    their steel.

And hosts like the locusts' swarm have swept upon me alone,
    and my hand it was that stemmed and gathered in one
    their spears.

Now am I as though I ne'er had mounted a noble steed,
    or called to my horsemen—Charge, gain space for our men
    to breathe !

Or bought for a wreath of gold the full skin of wine, or cried
    to true hearts at play,—Heap high the blaze of our beacon-
    fire ! "

Next I give a longer piece, already chosen out by
Mr. Poole for the same purpose, to show in what things
the Arab chief set his glory, and on what his heart
and love were fixed—

" A mountain we have where dwells he whom we shelter there,
    lofty, before whose height the eye falls back blunted :

Deep-based is its root below ground, while overhead there
    soars
    its peak to the stars of heaven whereto no man reaches.

A folk are we who deem it no shame to be slain in fight,
   though that be the deeming thereof of Salūl and Amir ;

Our love of death brings near to us our days of doom,
   but their dooms shrink from death and stand far distant.

There dies among us no lord a quiet death in his bed,
   and never is blood of us poured forth without vengeance.

Our souls stream forth in a flood from the edge of the
      whetted swords :
   no otherwise than so does our spirit leave its mansion.

Pure is our stock, unsullied : fair is it kept and bright
   by mothers whose bed bears well, and fathers mighty.

To the best of the uplands we wend, and when the season
      comes,
   we travel adown to the best of fruitful valleys.

Like rain of the heaven are we : there is not in all our line
   one blunt of heart, nor among us is counted a niggard.

We say nay when so we will to the words of other men :
   but no man to us says nay when we give sentence.

When passes a lord of our line, in his stead there rises straight
   a lord to say the say and do the deeds of the noble.

Our beacon is never quenched to the wanderer of the night,
   nor has ever a guest blamed us where men meet together.

Our Days are famous among our foemen, of fair report,
   branded and blazed with glory like noble horses.

Our swords have swept throughout all lands both east and
      west,
   and gathered many a notch from the steel of hauberk-
      wearers ;

Not used are they when drawn to be laid back in their sheaths
   before that the folk they meet are spoiled and scattered.

If thou knowest not, ask men what they think of us and
      them :
   not alike is he who knows and he who knows not.

The children of Ad-Dagyän are the shaft of their people's
      mill :
   around it turns and whirls, while they stand 'midmost "

Sir Charles Lyall's volume is, as I have said, a delightful one. He would do a great service to scholars and to lovers of poetry if he would give us a complete translation of the Hamāsa, thus doing, in our own tongue and in the light of fuller knowledge, what Rückert did more than fifty years ago for Germany.

CHAPTER III

HAVING tried to give some pictures of the life and
character of the desert Arabs, our task is now to
sketch the stages by which Arabia was prepared for
the coming of that great master-mind which was to
revolutionise it and conquer half the known world.
The task is not easy, nor is it altogether attractive.
The warring migrating tribes, whose meetings and
partings, feuds and friendships, make the web of
Arabia's history, are not less perplexing to follow in
their kaleidoscopic changes than the atoms from which
Epicurus fabled that the universe was framed. The
two leading threads through the mazes are found—first,
in the religious position of Mecca, established beyond
dispute from the earliest times of which we have any
record, and continued without interruption to the day
when the reforming exile, thrust out ten years before,
conquered and purified and transformed it to be the
spiritual capital of the new Faith; second, in the
migrations of the great Arab nations, caused partly by
that mysterious impulse which has in all ages driven

the human race to seek new homes and to subdue
lands unknown before, partly to causes which we can
more surely trace.

Arab tradition makes the great southern division of
the race to spring from a legendary head, Kahtān,
whose descendants, originally coming from the north,
flowed down like a great river, and established themselves all along the habitable coast-lands, by the Persian
Gulf on the east, Hadramaut on the south, and Yaman
on the shores of the Red Sea. Through Arabia flowed
to the west and north the riches of India as well as
her own products,—gold, frankincense, and myrrh;
ivory, ebony, and precious stones. So long as land-
carriage was the surer and safer, so long did the
desert-navies (as we may call them) bear the precious
bales along two main lines,—through Yaman and the
Hijāz to Syria and Egypt, and by the shores of the
Persian Gulf to Mesopotamia and the neighbouring
countries. Kahtān was the great ancestor of the
roaming Arabs, the carriers of the desert, whose
camels bore the precious merchandise; and Himyār
("the dusky"), fabled to be his brother, was pro-
genitor of the settled inhabitants. The great southern
kingdoms, of which Yaman was the chief, were Him-
yāritic; their language[1] is the *South Arabian*, divided
into three great branches, corresponding to the three
southern provinces (Yaman, Hadramaut, and Mahrāb),
and surviving now only in a multitude of rock-inscrip-
tions, ranging in date probably between the fourth
and seventh centuries of our era, thus dying with the
advent of Islām and the triumph of its tongue. Crossing over into Africa, we have the Geez and Abyssinian

[1] See Wright, *Comp. Gram. of Semitic Languages*, p. 28 and foll.

with its cognates. From the fertile land of Yaman
the stream of trade passed northward through the
barren Hijāz, and both Mecca and Medīna (which bore
its old name Yathrib till Muhammad fled thither
for refuge) were great emporiums of commerce. The
latter, as we shall see, had long been settled by a
powerful Jewish population, the fortunes of which
acted mightily on the new religion and the new polity
when the time came, while the former was the chief
centre and shrine of the idolatry which Muhammad
was to overthrow.

Yaman was the garden of Arabia, rich and fertile in
itself, though not capable of supporting the large
population which its flourishing through trade had
brought within its bounds. Its capital was Sanā; and
much of its prosperity was due to the great dam of
Mārib, where the fertilising waters from the mountain-
torrents were stored. When therefore Roman enter-
prise had to a large extent supplanted the old western
caravan trade by sea-borne traffic up the Red Sea, and
when also the great dam burst, and the stored waters
swept destroying over the lands which they used to
fertilise, then in the second century after Christ the
great Azdite branch of the Kahtānic race surged north
through the Hijāz, and east through Najd, leaving
behind, in successive stages, powerful clans of their
kindred, and founding on the Syrian and Persian
borders the kingdoms of Ghassān and Hīra. The
Himyārite kingdom of Yaman, relieved of its surplus
population, recovered its importance; its annals count
kings of valour and authority, one of whom is even
said to have "carried his conquests to the borders of
China," while another had his son murdered in Yathrib,

was then converted to Judaism, and established that
religion in Mecca. In the end of the third century a
Christian king ruled over the country, and in the
next, Christian churches were common; but the people
generally were partly Jewish and partly pagan, and
the Christian element had probably been introduced
and strengthened from the kingdom of Abyssinia, the
neighbouring state across the Red Sea. In 523 A.D.,
Dhu Nawās was king, a bigoted Jew, who massacred
the Christians of Najrān, so drawing upon him the
vengeance of Justin I., the Greek emperor. Abraha
moved against him from Abyssinia with a great host,
and slew him; Christianity was officially established
in the country, and a cathedral built at Sanā. An
attempt was made to replace the pagan worship at
Mecca by Christianity, and the Abyssinian army
advanced against the city. But the host was overwhelmed, and the commander perished; and 570, the
Year of the Elephant, so-called from the war-elephants
of the army, was marked by the triumph of paganism
and by the birth of Muhammad, the greatest iconoclast
the world has seen. Christian, and especially African,
rule, however, was hateful to the Himyārites; the
aid of Persia was called in, and, after some seventy
years of changeful fortune, the ancient kingdom of
Yaman became a dependency of that empire (597, the
year when St. Columba introduced Christianity into
the west of Scotland).

The other kingdoms which were founded to the
north of Arabia by the wave of migration from the
south, and which had constant traffic with and influence over the Hijāz, were Hīra and Ghassān. The
former, Hīra, was settled by an aggregation of tribes,

forced north and east by the Azdites from Yaman,—
rearing up a strong kingdom on the ruins of the
Persian Arsacid power. At first the kingdom was
divided between Khudhāites and Azdites, but soon the
former hived off to Syria, and the latter remained sole
owners. Civilisation came to them chiefly from Persia,
and they fell into a state of dependent alliance on that
empire. The early history of Hīra mingles strangely
with that of Rome, in its wars with Zenobia of Palmyra,
after whose fall rose the rival kingdom of Ghassān dependent on Rome (*i.e.* Constantinople), as Hīra was on
Persia. Christianity was introduced under Numān I.
early in the fifth century, and under his fostering
care became the dominant religion of the state, though
it is not certain that the king himself embraced it.
Under his successors the Christians were persecuted,
with the result of constant quarrels with Constantinople; but in 524 A.D. toleration was secured by the
efforts of Justin I., whose Abyssinian ally (as has been
told) overwhelmed the kingdom of Yaman about the
same time. The power of Yaman had decayed in
Central Arabia about this time, and the country fell
under the power of Hīra, as vassal of Persia. Then
ensued well-nigh a century of struggle with Ghassān, the
ally of Constantinople, with raids and plunder throughout Syria, till the bands of Hīra, the vanguard of
the Persian hosts, were hurled back by Belisarius
from the walls of Antioch. At length, in 605 A.D., the
dynasty was overthrown by the arms of Persia; a few
years of anarchy and confusion followed; the forces of
Persia were routed by an Arab confederacy in the
Valley of Zu Kār in 611 A.D., the very year when
Muhammad had assumed his prophetic mission,—and,

finally, between 628 and 631 A.D., the Central and Western tribes of Arabia threw off the alien yoke and cast in their lot with their kinsmen under the national Prophet-King.

The kingdom of Ghassān was founded under the shadow of the Roman power in the third century by an Azdite tribe long settled near Mecca. The two great Aus and Khazraj clans broke off, struck back southwards in the fourth century, and settled in Yathrib (Medīna), where they deprived the Jewish settlers of power. Christianity was introduced about the time of Constantine, and continued to be the state religion; the annals of the kingdom are made up of wars, forays, and revolts; it was shattered by Persian invasion in the beginning of the seventh century; and after some years of stout resistance to the armies of Islām, it also fell before them, and was absorbed in the growing empire.

Yaman, Hīra, and Ghassān, and the nomad tribes of Central Arabia,—these were the powers that acted upon the Hijāz from without, but it is not easy to measure the effect they produced. The religious power of Mecca as the immemorial shrine of pagan Arabia, the goal of its pilgrimages, the pantheon of its idols, was far greater; and the strong Jewish colony settled at Medīna, whose faith combined readily with the Abrahamic legend and myth of Mecca, was destined greatly to influence the new religious empire which Muhammad was to found,—so much so that Deutsch boldly affirms that "Islām is no more than Judaism *plus* belief in Jesus and in Muhammad." Let us now see what was the history of those two city-states.

The origin of Mecca is lost in antiquity. As far

back as we have any knowledge it was both great as a
commercial centre, and as a holy place still greater,—
for to it looked the devotion of all the scattered nations
of Arabia. Herodotus (iii. 8) mentions under a Greek
disguise the chief god Allāh, and refers to the worship
of the hosts of heaven and of sacred stones; while
Diodorus Siculus, four centuries later, speaks of a
" temple in this country (the eastern coast of the Red
Sea) greatly revered by all the Arabs." Mecca, also
called Becca,—as, in India, Bombay is with the natives
Mumbai, means a " meeting-place." The earliest settlement in the country appears to have been by tribes of
Ishmaelitish descent, together with their kinsmen the
Jurhamites. The chief object of ambition from the
beginning was the control of the Kaaba, the building
of which myth ascribed to Abraham by God's command,
after Hagar and Ishmael had settled in the valley; the
holy well Zemzem (the " bubbling spring ") had burst
up miraculously to supply the thirsty child's need;
and Hagar's distracted search for water has been from
time immemorial recalled at the annual sevenfold race
between Safâ and Marwa. Authentic history begins
in the first century B.C. with Adnān the Jurhamite,
back to whom Muhammad traced his lineage, but
beyond whom he declared there was no certainty. At
the great upheaval caused by the Azdite migration
from Yaman, the powerful Khudhāa confederacy
ousted the Maāddites (sons of Adnān) from power,
though these latter retained throughout some of the
chief offices of the sanctuary; and it was then that the
idols were placed in the Kaaba. In the fifth century,
Qusāi, the Quraish chief, from whose lineage in the
fifth generation sprang the prophet Muhammad, headed

a revolt against the Khudhāa power, and with the aid
of kindred tribes established his own. He gathered
up into his hands the reins of all civil and religious
authority, extended the city limits by cutting down the
grove that hitherto had been held sacred from human
dwellings, and brought together within its bounds
the scattered members of the Quraish tribe. He built
for the transformed and extended city a town-hall, the
centre of civil and social life, with an entrance on to
the Kaaba, whence were sent forth the bannered hosts
for war, where maidens of full age assumed the garb of
womanhood, and where the ceremonies of marriage were
performed. There, too, the elders of the city held high
counsel, all affairs of the public weal were determined,
and from it set forth, and to it returned the half-yearly
caravans on which Mecca mainly depended for its wealth.

To secure the quiet observance of the rites of pilgrimage, Arab tribal law had enforced peace during
four months of the year, the eleventh, twelfth, first,
and seventh. During these, all feuds were hushed, and
the deadliest foes met in mutual security. But the
religious chief of Mecca had the singular power of
substituting the second month of the year for the first
as a month of truce, the first then becoming common.
It may easily be seen how great was this power (called
Nasā, commutation), and how it might be abused, as
was the similar power of the pontifices of Rome in
regard to their religious calendar. This power, together with the starting of the pilgrims for Mount
Arafāt and Minā (Ijāza), providing them with food
and water (Rifāda and Siqāya), the custody of the
keys of the Kaaba (Hijāba),—all was vested in Qusāi.
The ceremonies of the pilgrimage were purely pagan:

3

the pilgrims threw off all clothing to make the mystic
sevenfold circuit of the Kaaba, symbolising perhaps
planetary motion, though strangely (and contrary to
almost universal practice in other religious ceremonies)
the circuit was made *against* the course of the sun;
they adored the many idols placed in and around the
Holy House; and they rapturously kissed the Black
Stone, of meteoric origin, symbol and centre of the
old stone-worship, one of the most widespread forms
of ancient superstition. The divinities most worshipped
were Allāh, the supreme god, Allāt (perhaps only a
feminine form of the former), who with Al Uzzā and
Manāt (a sacrificial stone) was fabled to be a daughter
of the Supreme Allāh; Hubal, the rain-god, Wadd or
Heaven, with others in shape of lion, horse, and eagle.
Hosts more there were, the whole number being no
less than 365 in Muhammad's day. Sacred stones are
scattered throughout Arabia, early native historians
say that they were carried from Mecca to represent
the Black Stone, and Palgrave found in Central Arabia
monoliths and stone-circles which reminded him of
Stonehenge and the *menhirs* of Brittany. But, besides
the gods, the tribes believed in *Jinns*, formed of fire as
mankind from clay, but otherwise of very similar
constitution though greater power; and their knowledge of a future life was vague and dim, and not
general. It was not uncommon for a camel to be
tied by the grave of a chief, with the idea, apparently,
that in the future life it would serve to carry the dead
man, as it had done in the world he had left.[1]

---

[1] Marco Polo in his *Travels* tells how in his day it was the custom
in Central Asia to slaughter hosts of men and women to swell the state
of a deceased Tartar chief.

The varying feuds and fights and fortunes of the tribes which dwelt in and roamed through Central Arabia need not be particularly traced. Powerful as many of them were, the curse of disunion was on them then, as it is again now that the national feeling created by Islām has long spent its force. Owning by turns the supremacy of Yaman or of Hīra, some of them professing Judaism or Christianity for a while, the most part remained pagan, and when the states on their borders had sunk into weakness, they resumed their old unfettered freedom, till the time came to unite them under the standard of the new Faith. One influence, however, which almost certainly had greatly contributed to enlighten Muhammad and to shape his beliefs, came from Central Arabia. The state of Najrān, lying between Yaman and Najd, and settled by the Hārith tribe (of Kahlānite stock), had been Christian- ised by Syrian missionaries in the fifth century or earlier, and Qās, one of their bishops and a famous orator, was heard by the future Prophet, when a youth, at the great yearly fair of Ukāz.

Medīna, according to Arab tradition, was originally settled by the Amalekites; but these gave way in very early times to Jewish invaders, driven from their own land (probably) by the national disasters wrought by Nebuchadnezzar, and later conquerors. Prominent among them were the Nazīr, Quraiza, and Qainuqāa tribes, whom we shall find again under Muhammad's rule. About 300 A.D. the Aus and Khazraj tribes, of Azdite stock, struck back south from their kindred in Ghassān, and at first lived on good terms with the Jews who had hospitably welcomed them. But when they grew in numbers and felt their power, they, about

the end of the fifth century, rose against their Jewish
partners in the government, massacred the chiefs, seized
the best of their lands, and reduced the tribes to subjection. The treachery and massacre was avenged by
Abu Kārib, a prince (possibly from Yaman), who slew
the leaders, and devastated the cultivated lands, but
had then to retire. Thereafter followed twenty years
of strife between the rival clans; a truce for half a
century; then renewed war, ending after a terrible
battle at Buāth in 616 A.D. (where the strength of the
Jews was divided between the contending tribes, and
desert allies joined in the fray), in the triumph of the
Khazraj, whose chief, Abdallah ibn Ubai, was about to
be raised to the kingship of Medīna, when the Exile
from Mecca changed the fortunes of the city, so beginning his great secular career.

The foregoing account shows that when Muhammad
appeared there was already spread throughout Arabia
much knowledge of faiths purer than the idolatry of
Mecca in which he was bred. The ebb or flow of Arab
migration and trade had kept up a constant connection
between Mecca and the stronghold of Jewish power in
Medīna to the north and Yaman in the south; the
influence of Christianity also (though sadly abused
and distorted) was pressing in from Abyssinia, from
Najrān, from Hīra, and from Ghassān, with the shadow
of the once mighty Eastern Roman Empire in the back-
ground; and the earliest history of Mecca was strangely
bound up with legends of Abraham and Ishmael. But
none of these had had power to move deeply the Arab
soul, and where Judaism and Christianity had both
failed, Muhammad succeeded with a strange mixture
of both, compounded by the alchemy of his own genius.

CHAPTER IV

Qusāi to Muhammad—Abd al Muttalib—Redemption of Abdallah—Strength of Idolatry in Mecca—" Muslims before
Islām "—Zaid the Sceptic—Birth of Muhammad, a Post-
humous Child—Adoption by Abd al Muttalib—His Fosterage
and Early Childhood—Death of his Mother—Legends of his
Infancy—His Youth—Marriage to Khadīja.

QUSĀI, as we have seen, refounded Mecca, greatly
enlarged its borders, gathered into it the whole Quraish
clan, regulated the city government, and gradually
possessed himself of all authority therein. He kept
this power as long as he lived, and when he died, full of
years and honours, left his whole authority to his eldest
son, Abd al Dār. A younger brother Abd al Manāf,
however, being of stronger character, enjoyed the real
power, and his four sons inherited their father's
authority. But the family of Abd al Dār asserted
themselves, and after much dispute the powers of
government were divided between the kinsmen:
Hāshim and his brothers, sons of Abd al Manāf, kept
the right of providing food and drink to the pilgrims,
and that of leadership in war; whilst the grandsons of
Abd al Dār had the keys of the Kaaba, the presidency
in the town hall, and the right of raising the banner.
Hāshim exercised his office with princely liberality,
and his example was followed by the other wealthy

Quraish; the splendour of the annual pilgrimage was enhanced, and the glory of Mecca exalted. He also, like an Arab Joseph, saved his people from starvation in years of sore famine, and earned their lasting gratitude. He established a regular system of caravans, two each year,—one in winter to Yaman and Abyssinia, and the other in summer northward to Syria; and he and his brothers made advantageous treaties with their foreign neighbours. His prosperous and honoured life was for a time troubled by the envy of his nephew Umaiya, for envy is the curse of the Arab mind, who challenged his supremacy, and being adjudged loser retired in wrath to Egypt, which strife is marked by historians as the beginning of that Umaiyad rivalry with the Hāshimites which was in after days to work such harm in Islām.

In his old age, Hāshim, on one of his trading journeys, met at Medīna a noble, capable lady named Salma, who had been divorced by her husband. He loved, and married her, and a great feast was made to her tribe of Khazraj and his Quraish relatives. After a short stay with her husband in Mecca, Salma returned to her father's house, where a son was born to her in 497 A.D. Hāshim died not long after in Syria, leaving his dignities to his brother Al Muttalib, who brought his nephew to Mecca as soon as he could leave his mother. The lad was noble and goodly to look upon, but the Meccans, fancying he was a newly-purchased slave, hailed him as Abd al Muttalib ("slave of Al Muttalib"), by which name he was ever afterwards known. Not without strife, which obliged him to call in the armed help of his mother's kindred, did Abd al Muttalib secure his patrimonial rights; and it took years to overcome the envy of his relatives. At length he triumphed, and rose to more than his father's dignity and power, attaining almost to the supremacy enjoyed by Qusāi; for he rediscovered and dug again, after centuries of disuse, the holy well Zemzem, whose abundant waters have ever since mainly supplied the city of Mecca, and the myriads of pilgrims that crowd to her sacred shrines. The god Hubal declared by the arrows of divination that Abd al Muttalib alone should own and control the well and the golden treasures found buried therein, and the grateful chief spent the gold in adorning and enriching the Holy House.

An interesting legend of sacrifice averted marks the story. In the struggles of his manhood Abd al Mutallib was at a disadvantage from having but one son, who aided him in his quest for the famous well. So he vowed to his god Hubal that, if he should be blessed with ten sons, he would sacrifice one of them to the deity. The ten sons were given him, and six daughters, and, when the sons were all grown up to manhood, the father cast lots before the oracle to choose out the victim. Abdallah, sixth and best beloved, was taken; but God had ordered otherwise. Again, it is said at the instance of one of his daughters, the father cast the lot, to see if the god would take a ransom of ten camels for the lad; but the human victim was still claimed. Similarly, twenty camels were offered, and rejected; then thirty, and forty; nor was it till one hundred had been staked that the lot set Abdallah free. The camels of the ransom were sacrificed, and their flesh divided to the people, save that Hāshim's brothers would not partake of it, and the father of Muhammad was redeemed. Abd al

Muttalib, like Hāshim his uncle, was attacked by his envious kinsman Harb son of Umayya, and, like Hāshim, was declared victor in the contest. He strengthened his power by an alliance with the Khudh-āites of Mecca, the treaty being solemnly laid up in the Kaaba; and his fame was raised to its height when, in 570, eight years before his death, the mighty Abyssinian host under Abraha, advancing to destroy the Kaaba, perished under a mysterious pestilence before the gates of the city, with a destruction so complete that but one escaped to tell the woeful tidings, and he fell dead before his master's throne as soon as the story was told! Now, some months ere this, Abdallah, like his uncle Hāshim, had wedded a lady of Medīna, Amīna, daughter of Wahbra, who was descended from Zuhra, brother of the great Qusāi. His aged father, with whom he was travelling, married at the same time Amīna's cousin, Hālah, by whom he became the father of Hamza, the "Lion" of Islām. Abdallah died at Medīna on his way home from Syria, at the early age of twenty-five, and some months later Amīna was comforted over his death by the birth of her son Muhammad, the mightiest Arab of all times.

It is clear that when Muhammad was born in 570, there was no decline of paganism or idol-worship at Mecca. There was no sense of unreality, such as at Rome made Cicero wonder that two augurs could meet with grave faces, and which breathes in the poetry of Horace and Ovid, scarcely less than in Lucretius. The greatness of Mecca was bound up with the devotion to the Kaaba; at no time had the temple been more famous, the yearly pilgrimages more widely popular; and the fame of Quraish princes, Qusāi, Hāshim, Abd

al Muttalib, and the rest, was based on their service to
the Holy House. There was no breaking up of Mecca's
paganism, to render the work of revolution easy.
Seekers after God and a purer faith there had been,
more numerous perhaps, certainly to us better known,
about this time than in former generations. Of these
four men are specially marked out, and Sprenger exalts
their quest after truth at Muhammad's expense; but
probably no great revolution in human affairs, whether
in the domain of thought or of action, has been effected
without some previous strivings that have come to
nothing, and it is the leader whose work is carried to
success, the man who toils and labours till he reaches
the goal, to whom is justly due the crown of a nation's
or a world's praise. That Muhammad owed something
to the teaching, to the example, or to the encouragement of the four may be admitted, but it is easy to
exaggerate the debt. It is, however, a very interesting
story that of these "Muslims before Islām," derived
from early Muhammadan history, and runs somewhat
as follows:—

On a certain day, when the men of Quraish were
gathered at a yearly feast to one of their idols, slew
sacrifices, and went about the Sacred House, four men
kept apart, and agreed to open their hearts to one
another. They were Waraqa, cousin of Muhammad's
first wife Khadīja; Ubaid Ullāh, son of Muhammad's
paternal aunt; Uthmān, son of Al Hawairik; and
Zaid, of the Adi family. And one of them said to
the others: "By God, ye see that our tribe knows not
the true religion. They have corrupted the faith of
Abraham, and worship a stone, which neither hears nor
sees, and can do neither good nor harm. Friends, seek

for yourselves, for ye are not in the right path." So
they went forth each his several way, to seek for the
true faith of Abraham,—which faith Muhammad in
after time professed to restore. Waraqa studied the
Christian scriptures, was penetrated by their truth, and
embraced Christianity: he was a learned man, and
copied out a large part of the Gospels. Ubaid Ullāh remained a sceptic till he accepted Islām at Muhammad's
preaching in Mecca. He married Umm Habība, a
daughter of Abu Sufiyān, also a convert, with whom
he went to Abyssinia with the first exile. There he
became a Christian, and would tell his fellow-exiles
that he had found the truth, after which they were
still groping. He died ere he could return, and his
widow afterwards became one of Muhammad's wives.
Uthmān went to Constantinople, where he also professed Christianity, and was highly honoured by the
Emperor. Thus of the four seekers after God three
found Him in Christ.

The fourth, Zaid, remained a sceptic to the end,
finding no faith to satisfy him. Renouncing his
ancestral beliefs, he forsook the worship of idols,
refused to eat what had been sacrificed to them, or
blood, or that which died of itself, and he condemned
the cruel custom of burying girls alive. In extreme
old age he warned the Quraish that he only among
them held the true faith of Abraham, and he prayed,
saying: "O Lord, if I knew in what form Thou
wouldest be worshipped, so would I worship Thee ;
but I know it not." And again he said that he had
cast away his idols, and the idols of his tribe, to
worship the All-Merciful Lord, that He might forgive
his sins. "Whoso fears God will not be lost. The

good shall have their abode in the gardens of paradise, but the wicked shall dwell with the fire. In life they shall not prosper, and after death they shall be in torment." "Truly I am Thy servant, O Lord; and to Thee I submit myself, Whom the earth obeys, and the fertilising rain-clouds." Zaid was for long prevented by his cousin Khattāb from wandering forth in search of the truth, but succeeded at length. He wandered through Mesopotamia and Syria, questioning monks and Rabbins concerning the faith of Abraham; but none could tell him of it, save one who bade him go back to his own land, "for there (said he) has arisen a Prophet who will restore that ancient faith." So he turned his steps homeward, but was murdered on the way;—and in later times Muhammad refused not to pray for Zaid, though at another time he told his followers that he was commanded not to pray for any but Believers, and was expressly forbidden to pray for his own mother.

Reference has been already made to the wondrous tales told in later times by the devotion of his followers, to enhance the glory of Muhammad; but the simple facts do not need any embellishment to heighten our admiration for the mighty work he did, whatever judgment we may have to pass on the character and motives of the man, or on the nature of the revolution he achieved. The tribe to which he belonged, the Quraish, had, in the two centuries before his birth, raised itself to undisputed pre-eminence in Mecca. All power, civil, religious, and military, so far as the nature of Arab life permitted, was gathered in their hands. They had, by the exercise of those virtues which were most highly esteemed in Arabia, won the

widest fame; they had strong family ties and alliance
both with the other chief city of the Hijāz, Medīna
(Yathrib), and with the Bedouin tribes of Central
Arabia; their commerce was regular, gainful, and far-
reaching; and they had treaties of friendship with
powers beyond the limits of the peninsula. Abd al
Muttalib, the venerable chief of the Quraish, surrounded
by his large family of sons and daughters, and held in
high honour for his past services, ruled in Mecca. The
Abyssinian invasion had failed in circumstances which
lent colour to the belief in supernatural aid, and the
central shrine of Arabian idolatry was secure against
foreign foes.

The chief and his well-beloved son Abdallah had, as
has been told, married at the same time, in the end of
the year 569, two cousins, of a noble house in Medīna,
not distantly related to themselves. To the aged Abd
al Muttalib was born Hamza, afterwards so famous in
Islām, and to the newly-widowed Amīna (August 20,
570 A.D.) was given the child Muhammad. Still, after
all these thirteen centuries, the pious pilgrim gazes
reverently on his birthplace in the *Shi'b Maulūd*, the
"Quarter of the Nativity," not half a mile from the
Kaaba. After her marriage with Abdallah, Amīna
had gone to her husband's city, while he had gone
northward with the Syrian caravan. On his return
he sickened and died at Medīna, leaving to his widow
and unborn son five camels, a flock of goats, and a
female slave, Umm Aiman or Baraka, who tended the
infant when born. The little property was not small
for an Arab in that age, and in no case would Abd al
Muttalib's grandson have been allowed to want for
anything which Mecca could furnish.

Immediately word had come of the child's birth, the glad grandfather carried him in his arms to the Holy House, gave thanks to God, and named him Muhammad, "the Praised." This and the other common name Ahmad, which has the same meaning, are both derived from the Arabic root *hamada*, "to praise"; and in his later years Muhammad, from these names, supported his claim to be the "prophet" foretold by our Lord Himself in the Gospels,—*periklytos* (famous or renowned) instead of *parakletos*, the Advocate or Comforter.

As was usual in Mecca, Muhammad was not nursed by his own mother, but given over to a slave woman of his uncle Abu Lahb, who had lately nursed Hamza. Though he was not long in her care, Muhammad ever after showed the utmost love and gratitude towards her, honouring and helping her while she lived, and her daughter (his foster-sister) after, till she also died, not many years before his own death.

Mecca, however, has always been unhealthy for children, and it was the general custom of the wealthy Arabs to send them away with foster-mothers to be reared in the free, pure air of the desert, amid the black tents, the horses, and the camels, which are the immemorial theme of Arab song, and where also the noble Arabic tongue has ever flourished in stainless vigour. So, in the autumn after his birth, Muhammad was given to Halima, a woman of the Bani Saad, who had come with others to receive the care of Meccan infants. She did not take him without reluctance, as the care of a fatherless child was less likely to be well rewarded than that of one whose parents were both living. She proved, however, most faithful to her trust, the infant was carefully and lovingly tended, and had

grown to healthy, vigorous childhood when, at the
end of five years, he was finally returned to his mother's
charge. Tradition delights to tell how Halīma and
her whole house were favoured by heaven while the
young Prophet dwelt with her. The donkey she rode,
lean and almost foundered when she came into Mecca,
recovered speed and condition on her homeward way ;
it had been a season of drought, and the flocks and
herds of the tribe were lean and athirst, but on Halīma's
return the pastures flourished, and the cattle throve ;
and she and hers prospered even beyond their fellows.
The child grew up strong and healthy, generally speaking, and his great physical strength and endurance in
after life prove the soundness of his constitution. Yet
he suffered from some mysterious ailment, and was
subject to occasional fits. These in all Eastern lands
have ever been looked upon as cases of possession, and
in Arabia the sufferer is believed to be possessed by
a Jinn, one of those spirits formed of fire with which
Bedouin fancy has peopled the waste places of the
earth,—and to whom belong—

> " Those airy tongues which syllable men's names [1]
> In rocks, in plains, in barren wilderness."

It was, and still is, usual not to wean Arab children
for the long period of two years, and at the end of that
time, Halīma seems to have taken her foster-child to
his mother, and to have brought him back to the tents
for a like period more. At the end of the fourth year,
however, both Halīma and her husband were alarmed
by a fit which took the child; so they carried him

[1] Again Marco Polo witnesses for us to the many spirits that in his
time haunted the deserts of High Tartary (Yule's *Marco Polo*).

back to Mecca, intending to rid themselves of the charge altogether. But they were induced to resume it for another year, after which the boy Muhammad finally returned to his grandfather's house.

The occasion of Muhammad's first fit has been transmuted by the devout fancy of his followers into a miraculous cleansing of his heart from the stain of sin. It is related that he said to his anxious foster-mother that two men in shining raiment had thrown him to the ground, opened his breast, and taken out the heart and chief organs, yet without any pain; the organs were then washed in pure water, and from the heart was taken the black seed of sin, and then all was replaced. Such is the material form given to the allegory used by Muhammad in Sura 94 of the Qurān, —"Have we not opened thy breast?" In this, again, we see an Arabic version of the Psalmist's prayer,— "Create in me a clean heart, O Lord!"

The speech of the Sons of Saad was famous for its purity, and in later times Muhammad boasted that he was the "most perfect Arab, sprung from the tribe of Quraish, and speaking the tongue of the Bani Saad." His affectionate nature ever acknowledged the ties of fosterage, and when in a year of drought Halīma visited him in Mecca after his marriage to the wealthy Khadīja, he presented her to his wife, and that generous lady sent her away happy with the gift of a noble riding camel and a flock of forty sheep. Many years later, her daughter came to him in Medīna, and was treated with the greatest honour and affection; and when her tribe had lost many captives to him in an expedition against Tā,if, they redeemed themselves by reminding him of his childhood's days among them.

Over and over again in the story of Muhammad's life
we shall find how tender was his nature, how quick his
affections, and shall wonder the more at the few dark
passages where he showed himself without ruth or pity.

The year after his return to Mecca, Muhammad spent
under his mother's care, and at the end of that time she
desired to show him to his kinsfolk in Medīna.   So
she set forth with the boy and his nurse Umm Aiman,
and stayed in the city for a month, in the house where
her husband had died.   That month Muhammad never
forgot, and not many years before his own death he
told his companions the names of his playmates at that
time, and the games at which they played.   The memory
of those days was ever sweet to him, deepened by the
tragedy that so soon followed ; for, on their homeward
way to Mecca, sickness fell on Amīna, and she died at
Abwā when but half their journey was done, and there
she was buried ; and the faithful Umm Aiman took the
little orphan home, where the aged chief of Mecca
welcomed him.   The loss of his mother, the only parent
he had known, was a deep grief to the sensitive child's
heart, and his love and reverence for her never wore out.
More than fifty years later he turned aside to her grave,
as he went on his pilgrimage to Hudaibiya, and he wept
over it ; and his companions wept with him, and asked
the cause of his tears.   And he said he wept for tender
memory of his mother, and because the Lord had forbidden him to pray for her, inasmuch as she had died in
unbelief.   It is a scene full of pathos, the old man
weeping for the mother he had loved and lost in early
childhood, and shutting her out from what he thought
the grace of his intercession because she had not believed
in his prophetic mission.

So long as Abd al Muttalib lived, the boy was tenderly cared for. The old chief delighted in the child's company, shielded him from all annoyance, and treated him as the son of his old age. But two years later he also died, leaving his orphan grandson to the guardianship of Abu Tālib, a worthy successor, to whose firm and unwavering support through many stormy years Muhammad owed his very life, threatened as it was by the hatred of most of the Quraish, when he had broken with idolatry and claimed to be the Prophet of Allāh. The fresh bereavement was a heavy blow to Muhammad, but doubtless there mingled with his grief a proud memory of his grandfather's high character and great fame, which might well stir him to dreams of ambition. For the time, however, the fortunes of the family suffered eclipse. Several of Abd al Muttalib's sons were dead, his splendid hospitality had greatly diminished his wealth, and the riches and power of the clan had in large part passed to the descendants of Abd al Manāf.

Of the life of Muhammad for many years after this, till the date of his marriage, at the age of twenty-five, with Khadīja, scarcely anything is certainly known. He grew up under the care and protection of his uncle Abu Tālib, surrounded by the atmosphere of the best Arab life, and steeped (we may not doubt) in the family worship of idols, with which their rank and importance had been from the days of Qusāi so closely bound up. Late traditions, manifestly without any foundation in fact, have adorned (or defaced) a childhood and youth that were no doubt happy and uneventful with legendary foreshadowings of his future greatness, prophecies Jewish and Christian, by learned Rabbis and pious hermits, of the prophet that was to come last into the world,

4

to perfect and seal the revelation of God's will and purposes to mankind. Trees bowed in homage, clouds shaded him miraculously as he journeyed with the caravans, and stones cried out in thankfulness and praise as he passed.

In the legendary history of his childhood, by an obvious afterthought, Muhammad from his earliest years is shown constantly and strongly protesting against every form of idolatry, and this we may be sure is wholly untrue. He no doubt went with his uncles, sometimes with one, and sometimes with another, on the half-yearly trading expeditions (though tradition records only two such journeys), and his strong, observant, meditative mind would be fed from all springs of knowledge that came in his way. He would learn something of the true doctrines of both Judaism and Christianity, and the Qurān shows clearly that at some time or other of his life he gained a wide knowledge of the extravagance of Talmudic legend, and much also of apocryphal Christian fable. His family connection with Medīna also, and the constant passage through it when he went with the Syrian caravan, would give him special opportunities of learning from the Jews, and of observing the political and religious rivalries which he afterwards so skilfully turned to account. Certainly too he was present at the annual fairs held in the neighbourhood of Mecca, of which the chief was at Uqāz, where the poets and orators strove for the praise of an audience not less critical than those which decreed the prizes in Athens at the Great Dionysia. There his fancy was fed with the strange Arab tales, and his heart fired with the praise of valour, endurance, and high purpose, and his ear grew familiar with the strongest and most subtle harmonies of the noble Arab tongue,

with which he was to witch his world. Yet he himself
was no poet, at least so far as metrical composition is
concerned, and was strong in condemnation of poets and
poetry, though he was always fully alive to their great
power over the Arab mind, and was too wise not to make
use of their services when he could. At Uqāz too he
heard the fervent Christian preaching of Qās, the bishop
of Najrān, and might well have embraced the Christian
faith but for two causes—his stubborn family pride, and
the corruptions of that faith which he saw on every side
of him. Had he embraced Christianity, the world would
have had one religion less, and the calendar of saints
might have held one name more![1]

In truth very little that is certain is recorded of
Muhammad previous to his marriage with Khadīja.
He enjoyed a high character among the citizens, and
nothing stands against his name. As a youth he tended
the flocks, an occupation which was congenial to his
mild and reflective character; and he appealed to the
fact that (as he alleged) no prophet had been sent who
had not been a shepherd or a herdsman. This was true,
no doubt, of Moses and of David, but not of the greater
number of his forerunners, as he called them. Sprenger
draws, from the fact of his employment as a shepherd,
conclusions unduly harsh as to his lack of energy and
force of character. Against this must be set the fact
that he was one of the leading spirits in the *Hilf-ul-
Fuzūl*, a confederation bound together by oath (Hilf) to
right the wrongs of any, bond or free, who might be
injured while in Meccan territory. The league was
formed among the descendants of Hāshim and Muttalib,
with some allied families, and exercised a strong moder-

[1] This thought is Sir W. Muir's.

ating influence. When he was about twenty-five
years of age, Abu Tālib arranged that his nephew and
ward, who must have been favourably known for
honesty and skill in trading, should take charge in a
caravan going to Syria of the goods of the wealthy
Khadīja, a lady related to them. She gladly agreed to
give her young kinsman four camels as his hire, double
what she gave to others; he conducted the venture with
prudence and success, and on his return Khadīja, delighted with the further knowledge she gained of his
character, no less than with his winning presence and
comely person, made advances that ended in their
marriage,—a happy union indeed for Muhammad, who
lived with her in perfect and undivided love till she
died twenty-five years later, in 620 A.D. She had
been already twice married, and had borne two sons
and a daughter to her husbands. At the time of her
marriage to Muhammad she was forty (lunar) years old,
as we should say, thirty-six, and to him also she bore
two sons and four daughters. Both the sons died in
early childhood, but the daughters all grew up to
womanhood, though only one of them—Fātima—survived her father, being the wife of Alī, his cousin and
faithful follower, afterwards third Khalīfa, from whom
all the numerous Sharīfs and Sayyids trace their
descent. Curiously enough, it seems that Khadīja could
not marry without the consent of her father, who was
averse to the match. So she plied him with wine till
he yielded, and when he awoke to find the marriage accomplished, he was too wise to interfere further. Considering how much he thus owed to the fruit of the
vine, one might think Muhammad's stern laws against
it savoured of ingratitude!

The marriage with Khadīja gave Muhammad that ease of circumstances which he needed, freedom from the cares of daily life, the stay and comfort of deep mutual love, which for twenty-five years never failed him. His wife retained the management of her wealth in her own capable hands, so that his mind was not burdened with the care of it; whatever he needed was liberally supplied. He was able, by adopting his young cousin Alī, to discharge a part of the debt he owed to Abu Tālib, who had now fallen into straitened circumstances; and it was Khadīja who bought and presented to him Zaid, whom he set free and adopted as his son, and who was one of the first, boldest, and most loyal of his followers. In spite of the great difference in age, Muhammad's love for Khadīja never wavered; when she was removed by death, after sharing with him for years the trials and the reproach of the early times of his preaching, he mourned her deeply; and, in later days, his favourite wife, the sprightly, clever, winsome Ayesha, said she had never been so jealous of any woman as "that old, withered, toothless" Khadīja. But when she petulantly asked if she had been the only woman worthy of his love, Muhammad answered gravely and tenderly: "She believed in me when none else did, she comforted me when sad and downhearted, and she alone of my wives bore me children"; and on another occasion he said, "The best of women in Paradise are Mary the daughter of Imrān (the Virgin Mary) and Khadīja the daughter of Khawailid."

CHAPTER V

FOR ten years Muhammad's life flowed on outwardly
in happy obscurity. If his heart was disquieted over
the idolatry of his people, he felt no call to witness
against it, and at the end of that time he took a chief
part in rebuilding its central fane. The Kaaba was
threatened with destruction by a flood, and the
alarmed Quraish resolved to rebuild it. The work
was divided among the leading families, and went on
in harmony till the holy Black Stone was to be put in
its place. Then strife broke out among the chiefs, each
claiming for himself the high honour of putting the
Stone in position. But as they sat debating the point,
it was determined to accept the decision of the first
who should enter the temple precincts. This was
Muhammad, hailed as "Al Amīn," the Trusty, who
directed that four of the chief men should hold the
corners of a sheet, and so lift the Stone to the level
where it was to be built into the wall, and then he
guided it to its resting-place, and the dispute was
happily ended.

But now the time was coming when he was to break finally with the idolatry in which he had been brought up, and with which was bound up so much of the greatness of his family and his tribe. Much given to solitary musings, a habit which was fed and fostered by his years of shepherd life, he was wont to pass long periods in retirement among the hills and ravines in the neighbourhood of Mecca. Of these one in particular, a cave on Mount Hīra, known in Islām as the Mount of Light, was a favourite resort. It was a lofty, barren, conical hill two or three miles north of the city, and thore too Zaid the Sceptic had had his hermit's abode, when he also had renounced the idolatry of his fore-fathers. And when, in his fortieth year (probably), Muhammad, as his wont was, was spending the month of Rajab, one of the months of peace, in spiritual wrestlings, communing with his own heart, and earnestly seeking for guidance, in the midst of his "prayers and supplications" (Ar. Tahannoth = Heb. Tehinnoth, according to Deutsch's brilliant explana-tion), the light of revelation seemed suddenly to burst upon him. In the middle of the night, on the "blessed night Al Qadr" (power, might), a glorious angel roused him from sleep; three times the mighty voice sounded in his ear, and three times the powerful constraining grasp was laid upon him. Twice he refused the mission, but the third call broke down every barrier,— and he took up the message from his Lord, brought by the angel Gabriel, the same who had brought down the glad tidings of the Annunciation to the Virgin Mary. Probably no one will doubt that the whole story was woven by Muhammad, perhaps only half consciously, out of fragments dimly remembered of

Jewish and Christian records. The first message ran, graven as with a pen of iron on the tablet of his heart (to use his own phrase)—

> "Cry (or 'Read') in the name of thy Lord,—
> Who created man from clots of blood!
> Cry, for thy Lord is most bountiful,
> Who has taught the use of the pen,
> Taught man what he knew not!"

Muhammad was terrified at the vision, and returned to Khadīja in great trouble. Then, as ever, she comforted him, soothed his fears lest he should be "possessed," and pointed to his blameless life as proof that God's purposes with him could only be good.

On this first vision followed a long period, which tradition sometimes extends even to seven years, but which is generally held to have been two, during which the visions were interrupted. During this time Muhammad continued his solitary musings and prayers, seeking for light. Often anguish of mind made his brain reel, and he sought to take his own life by casting himself headlong down a precipice. But ever, as he told the tale, Gabriel stayed him from the rash act, though the final seal of his mission was withheld. What really happened in this mysterious interval must always be matter of conjecture. Sprenger, who altogether rejects Muhammad's claim to originality, and has but small belief in his sincerity, has no doubt that the "revelation" was only a veil for the resolve to search the Scriptures of the Jews and Christians, and that the interval was used in reading, hearing, and being taught in them. Muir

again collects some of the short, passionate, lyrical out-
bursts which, now preserved in the Qurān, he believes
to be prior to the claim to preach, and assigns them
to this time.   Neither explanation is free from ob-
jection, nor probably would any other be; the evidence
rests wholly on Muhammad's own report, and partakes
of the confusion of an agonising mind.   We shall
escape a good deal of perplexity by following Muslim
tradition, remembering that the Quraish always declared that Muhammad's teaching was partly derived
from foreign secret prompters, and partly from his
own heated imagination.   The question whether he
could or could not read is not of great importance,
and is at this date insoluble.   He always called himself the "Unlettered Prophet," and appealed to the
perfect harmony and eloquence of his Qurān as being
therefore a miracle, sufficient to prove his prophetic
mission.   Inability to read would not have been a bar
to acquisition of knowledge, and a retentive memory
(such as was common in Arabia) would secure it.
During this period of mental strain, Muhammad's state
gave his friends much concern; they feared he was
verging on insanity, and he himself at times shared
that fear.   In the days of his early preaching, his
fellow-citizens scoffed at him as a poet, a visionary, a
soothsayer, and one possessed; and against these re-
proaches he constantly protests in the Qurān, declaring with passion that he is a Prophet sent of God,
inspired and taught by Him alone, and every word of
command, or story, or exhortation has (expressed or
implied) the preface—"Say!" *i.e.* in the name of the
Lord.   Every word of the Qurān, as Muhammad
taught, existed from all eternity, the Word of God,

engraven on the Preserved Tablet, and is chanted in heaven by angels and archangels and by the prophets of olden time.

At the end of the period of "remission," or suspension of messages from on high, Muhammad was again visited by the angel Gabriel, who gave him the divine command to preach to his people, assured him of the truth of his message, and dispelled doubts and fears of the reality of his commission. Pious fable tells how his heart was again purified, to make it fit for the divine message; but it is left to us to imagine how gradually there took shape in his mind the cardinal doctrines of the faith which thenceforward he preached, the existence of one God only, Almighty, absolute Ruler over all, whose decrees are fixed from all eternity, with whom none may intercede save by His permission, merciful and compassionate, righteous, yet forgiving; the certainty of the resurrection and final judgment of all mankind, when sin shall be punished and righteousness rewarded; the mission of Muhammad as the Apostle of God, the acceptance of whose teaching was the sole and all-sufficient condition of salvation, and the rejection of it the only unpardonable sin. The guilt and folly of idol-worship, the infinite importance of the future life,—these were the two prime elements of Muhammad's early message.

When these central truths had taken full possession of his mind, when he had persuaded himself that truly he was called of God to preach the true faith to his people and to the world,—his doubts all vanished, and he clothed the circumstances of his call to preach in the following story. As he wandered in perplexity in the mountains and rocks about Mount Hīra, where the first revelation had come down to him, and despaired because no more had been vouchsafed, suddenly a mighty voice from heaven called him. He looked up, and lo! Gabriel sat upon a throne between heaven and earth; and he said, "Verily, O Muhammad, thou art the Prophet of God, and I am Gabriel." Comforted and strengthened he went home; but the conflict of emotions had exhausted him, and he prayed Khadīja to wrap him in a mantle; and, as he thus lay, the call came in the words of the 74th Sūra (Chapter of the Qurān): "O thou that are covered, rise up and preach, and extol thy Lord! Make clean thy garments, and flee all abomination! Grant not favour to gain increase, and wait for thy Lord! When the trumpet shall sound, verily that day is a day of dread, terrible for them that misbelieve!" Such was the message that sent Muhammad forth on his mission, from which henceforward he never swerved, though once only for a very brief time he faltered. It is probable that in the interval between the first and the second revelation he had sought converts among the people, had failed, and had fallen into a state of despondency like that of the prophet Elijah when, fainting under the persecution of Jezebel, he prayed that he might die, "for I am not better than my fathers," "I, even I only am left." There came also, along with the command to preach, the comfortable assurance that God was with him—"By the brightness of day, and the darkling night, thy Lord hath not forsaken thee, neither hath He hated thee! Verily the life to come is better than that which is now, and at the last He shall give thee that wherewith thou shalt be well pleased? Did not He find thee an orphan, and care for thee; erring, and He guided thee; needy, and He enriched thee? Wherefore oppress not the orphan, and deny not the beggar, and show forth the mercies of thy Lord!" And again he was strengthened by the memory of past deliverance, and urged thereby to labour for his Lord (S. 94): "Have not we enlarged thy breast? and removed from thee the load that galled thy back? and exalted thy fame? Verily with difficulty is ease! verily with difficulty is ease! And when thou art at leisure, then toil and thirst after thy Lord!"

Thus heartened and strengthened, Muhammad asserted his prophetic claims. He had at first but small success in his mission, and the citizens for the most part scoffed at and reviled him. But slowly he gathered about him a small company of devoted followers, men and women, freemen and slaves,—and the best proof of his sterling character and absolute sincerity at this time is to be found in the fact that his first converts were those who knew him best, and whose eyes no weakness of character could escape, nor cloak of hypocrisy hide his true nature. First and best was his faithful wife, Khadīja, whose belief in him upheld his courage when all was dark, and with her doubtless his daughters grew up in the faith. Next, rivals for the honour of first disciple, came his young cousin Ali, whose fiery zeal and loyal spirit ever stood the prophet in such good stead, and Zaid, son of Hārith, whom he had set free from servitude and adopted as his son, and who remained bound to him by cords of love more firmly than by any forced bondage,—and who, in later years, made for him the utmost sacrifice a man can make, that of a cherished wife surrendered to

his Master's love. Of Ali it is told that he was Muhammad's companion when they worshipped Allāh secretly
together, and his father, Abu Tālib, who had heard of
his nephew's new doctrine, came suddenly upon them.
"What, my nephew," he said, "is this new faith I see
thee follow?" And he answered, "This, my uncle, is
the religion of God, and of His angels, and of His
prophets; the religion of Abraham. The Lord hath
sent me an apostle to His servants; and none is so
worthy as thou to be called to assist the Prophet of the
Lord." Abu Tālib could not forsake in his old age the
religion of his fathers; but he promised Muhammad his
fullest protection, and bade his son Ali follow him, "for
he will lead thee into no evil way." But the most important of the earliest converts was Abu Bakr, son of
Kuhāfa, one of the chief men of Mecca—wealthy,
generous, and of very high character. Singularly
truthful, mild, upright, and firm, he is known as *Al
Siddīq*, "the Truthful," as Muhammad himself was *Al
Amīn*, "the Trusty." His name Abu Bakr [1] means
"Father of the Virgin," that is, of Ayesha, the only
wife of Muhammad who had not been previously
married, and who at the time of her father's conversion
was but a child of two or three years old. To Abu
Bakr, afterwards Muhammad's first successor, the debt
of Islām is very great, though Sprenger perhaps ex-
aggerates it; and of him Muhammad said: "I never
invited any to the faith who displayed not hesitation
and perplexity, excepting only Abu Bakr; but he,
when I offered him Islām, tarried not, nor was per-
plexed." They had long been friends, were of almost

[1] The sobriquet has completely displaced the real name, Abd al
Kaaba.

equal age, and lived in the same quarter of the city.
He was short of stature, fair, and of delicate features,
with a high forehead, and keen, deep-set eyes. He
greatly helped the infant faith by the use he made of
his wealth in redeeming from bondage and ill-usage the
many slave converts, among whom most notable was
Bilāl, whose mighty voice called the faithful to public
prayer. Uthmān, afterwards third Khalifa, came next,
a merchant also like Abu Bakr; and Abd al Rahmān
and Talha. Muhammad cemented the ties of disciple-
ship by those of affinity: to Zaid he gave his nurse,
Umm Aiman, and to Ali and Uthmān respectively his
daughters Fātima and Rukāya. All told, however, at
the end of three years of private preaching, the followers of the new faith numbered no more than from
thirty to forty. But the people of Mecca, and not least
Muhammad's own near kinsfolk, bitterly opposed his
new doctrine,—and its worst foes were two of his uncles,
Abu Jahl and Abu Lahb ("Fathers of *Folly* and of
Fire"), the latter of whom is with his wife singled out
for a special chapter of cursing, being the only person,
besides Zaid [1] and the Prophet [2] himself, who is men-
tioned in the Qurān by name. The short chapter is
characteristic of Muhammad's fierce spirit, and may be
quoted entire—

" In the name of God, merciful and gracious !
Abu Lahab's two hands shall perish, and he shall perish !
His wealth shall not avail him, nor that which he hath earned !
He shall broil in a fire that flames,[3] and his wife carrying faggots !
    —on her neck a cord of palm fibres."   (PALMER, S. 111.)

---

[1] In respect of the divorce of his wife, that she might be married to
the Prophet.

[2] Muhammad is *named* in the Qurān four times.

[3] A pun on his name.

Having now got together a small and devoted band of followers, Muhammad took a further step in advance. The doctrines he had so far preached were, he contended, no new thing; he was not the preacher of a new religion, but the restorer and reviver of the ancient faith of Abraham, forgotten or overlaid by the idolatry and superstitions that had grown up and choked the pure worship to which the great founder had dedicated the Holy House of Mecca, the Kaaba. The guardianship of the fane was in the hands of his kindred, its purification was what he had greatly at heart, the ties of blood counted for much among the Arabs, and he thought the time had come when he might with some hope of success preach more publicly, but especially appealing to his own kinsfolk, to depart from idolatry, and to follow the old pure faith which he proposed. He did not, of course, give any such reasons as the above for his action. The angel Gabriel had, he said, brought down a further revelation of God's will, of His merciful purposes to the Prophet's kindred, for whose welfare he was so deeply concerned, —" Arise and warn ! Publish that which hath been commanded thee, and withdraw from the idolaters. We will take part with thee against the scoffers, and them who join other gods with God. Invoke thou no other god with Him, lest thou become of them that are appointed for punishment. Preach thou to thy kinsmen, thy near ones; spread the wings of protection over them that believe and follow thee, and say: I bring you a clear message."

In obedience to these commands, Muhammad first preached openly to the Quraish from the little hill of Al Safā, the same sacred eminence which is the scene to this day of preaching at the annual pilgrimage. He followed this up by a general invitation to the family of Abd al Muttalib to an entertainment, after which he intended to deliver his solemn message. A first attempt was defeated by Abu Lahb, his uncle, but on the second he secured his audience and fulfilled his mission. Thus he spake: "I know no man in the land of Arabia who can lay before his kinsfolk a more excellent offer than that which I now make to you. I offer you the happiness both of this world and of that which is to come. God Almighty hath commanded me to call mankind unto Him. Who, therefore, among you will second me in that work, and thereby become my brother, my vice-gerent, my Khalifa ('successor')?" At once impetuous Ali, whom we may call the Peter of Islām, sprang to his feet and exclaimed: "I, O Apostle of God, will be thy minister (wazīr). I will knock out the teeth, tear out the eyes, rip up the bellies, and cut off the legs of all who shall dare to oppose thee." Then Muhammad embraced him before the assembled guests, and said: "This is my brother, my deputy, my Khalifa: hear then, and obey him." Then the whole company broke into laughter, and told the venerable Abu Tālib that he must now be obedient to his own son!

It is of the feast on this occasion that is told the story of a miracle of feeding, which may serve as a specimen of the tales with which later ages embellished the Prophet's early career, regardless of his own disclaimer of miraculous power. Ali, who had been directed to furnish the meal, had not been able to provide for more than one guest; but though forty were present, all ate, and were filled. The prominent place given on this occasion to Ali, and especially the naming of him as "Successor," points to invention by Shiah partisans in later times; but the main fact of the first public preaching being addressed to a gathering of the family is in itself likely, and is quite in accordance with Muhammad's methods.

Notwithstanding this repulse, he must have derived encouragement from the meeting, for he went on to more boldness in his preaching. He denounced the folly of trusting to dumb idols, who could neither hear nor see, and had no power to help their worshippers, and he solemnly warned them of the judgment to come. He appealed to his character among them, and asked if they would believe him if he had warned them of the approach of an earthly foe; and they answered, "Yea, verily, for we have ever found thee a speaker of truth." Then he said, "Of a truth Allāh hath appointed me his Apostle to you all! I swear by Allāh that there is no God besides Him! Ye will all die as though ye fell asleep, and ye will be raised again as though ye awoke. For all your deeds ye must give an account, and ye shall be punished or rewarded according to your deserts." But few heeded him, and his uncle, Abu Lahb, derided him, saying, "Our kinsman is possessed, care not for him." And thereafter, when he passed through the streets, they would say, "Lo, the man who gives news about heaven, and with whom the angels of God hold converse!" Yet he went on with his preaching, and boldly taught that their forefathers, who had died without a knowledge of his mission, were condemned to the pains of hell.

Muhammad went on with his teaching, and sought specially to influence and win over the leaders of the

5

people. It is to this time that is assigned a pleasing
instance of that humility and real kindliness of nature
which were of such use to him throughout his life. As
one day he was earnestly pressing his mission on some
of the chief men of Mecca, a blind man, Abdallah, son
of Umm Maqtūm, came up and importuned him to
recite from the Qurān to him. The Prophet turned
impatiently away from him, but soon after repented of
the harshness, and produced against himself the sharp
rebuke embalmed to this day in the sacred Book—

" The Prophet frowned and turned his back, for that there came
to him a blind man !

But what would make thee know whether haply he may be
purified ? or may be mindful and the reminder profit him ?

But as for him who is wealthy, thou dost attend to him, and
thou dost not care that he is not purified ; but as for him
who cometh to thee earnestly fearing the while, from him
thou turnest away !

Nay, verily ! The Qurān is a memorial, and whoso pleaseth
will remember it,—

In honoured pages exalted, purified, in the hands of noble,
righteous scribes [1] ! " (S. 80).

Ever thereafter Muhammad showed the blind man
special respect and honour, greeting him with the
words, " Welcome the man for whose sake my Lord
rebuked me ! " and in the days of his power he twice
made him governor of Medīna.

Thus gradually was growing the number of Muhammad's adherents, and the fears of the Quraish increased
day by day. They tried again, as they had tried
before, to detach Abu Tālib from him, but in vain.
They then plied him with temptation. One day, as he
sat in the enclosure of the Kaaba, one of their number,

[1] The angels.

Utba, whose own younger brother had joined the new faith, sat down beside him, and said—

"O son of my friend, you are a man eminent both for your great qualities and for your noble birth. Although you have thrown the country into turmoil, created strife among families, outraged our gods, and taxed our forefathers and wise men with impiety and error, yet would we deal kindly with you. Listen to the offers I have to make to you, and consider whether it would not be well for you to accept them."

Muhammad bade him speak on, and he said—

"Son of my friend, if it is wealth you seek, we will join together to give you greater riches than any Quraishī has possessed. If ambition move you, we will make you our chief, and do nothing save by your command. If you are under the power of an evil spirit, which seems to haunt and dominate you so that you cannot shake off its yoke, then will we call in skilful physicians, and give them much gold that they may cure you."

"Have you said all?" asked Muhammad; and then, hearing that all had been said, he poured forth on his amazed listener the 41st chapter of the Qurān—

"Lo, a revelation from the Merciful and Gracious, a book whose signs (or verses) are clearly set forth, an Arabic Qurān for the people who know, a herald of glad tidings and a warning. But most of them turn aside and hear not, and say, 'Our hearts are veiled from that to which thou dost call us, and in our ears is dulness, and between us and thee there is a veil! Act thou, we too shall act.'[1] Say, 'I am but a mortal like yourselves, I am inspired that your God is one God;

---

[1] *I.e.* Go thy way, and we will go ours.

then go straight to Him, and ask forgiveness of Him; and woe to the idolaters, who give not alms, and in the hereafter disbelieve.' [1]

" Verily, those who believe and do right, for them is a hire that is not grudged.

" Say, ' What, do you really misbelieve in Him who created the earth in two days, and do you make peers for Him,—who is the Lord of the worlds ? ' "

Then, after warning his hearer by the stories of ancient Ad and Thamūd, destroyed for rejecting the prophets sent to them, he continued—

" And the day (shall come) when the enemies of God shall be gathered into the fire, marshalled along; until, when they come to it, their hearing and their eyesight and their skin shall bear witness against them, and shall say, ' He created you at first and unto Him shall ye return, but ye thought God knew not of your doings, and that thought has been your ruin.'

" Them who misbelieve will We make to taste keen torment, and the recompense of the enemies of God is the fire : for them is an eternal abode therein,—a requital for their gainsaying Our signs.

" But those who say, ' Our Lord is God, and walk uprightly,' upon them do the angels descend (and say), ' Fear not, nor be grieved, but receive the glad tidings of paradise promised unto you : and ye shall have therein what your souls desire.'

" Of His signs are the night and the day, and the sun and the moon.   Worship not the sun, neither the moon ; but worship God who hath created them, if ye be His servants.   But if they be too big with pride—yet those

[1] It is God who speaks.

who are with thy Lord celebrate His praises by night
and day, and are never weary.

" And this too is a sign : thou seest the earth faint,
and when we send down rain upon it, it stirs and swells ;
verily, He who quickens it will surely quicken the
dead ; verily, He is mighty over all.

" Whoso doeth right it is for his own soul, and whoso
doeth evil it is against it, for thy Lord is not unjust
towards His servants."

Such was the sermon preached to Utba, of which
only an abridgment can be given ; and he went back
awed to those who had sent him, and thereafter
followed Muhammad. For he said he had heard such
things as came not to his ears before, not vision nor
poetry, but a clear message from God. Further over-
tures were made, and repulsed ; and then recourse was
had to stronger measures. It does not appear, however,
that Muhammad himself and his chief followers had to
bear more than insult and social ostracism : torture fell
on slaves, and severe hardship on those who had no
powerful protectors in Mecca. And here it was that
the wealth and pitiful nature of Abu Bakr served to
foster the infant Church of Islām, redeeming the slaves
and aiding the destitute.

CHAPTER VI

THE strife between Muhammad and his townsfolk
grew rapidly more bitter. Persecution and violence
were met by defiance and threats; but, in the fourth
year of his preaching, Muhammad took up his abode in
the house of Arqam, an early convert, and made it a
meeting-place for all converts and inquirers (613 A.D.).
Here the little band grew, and Muhammad's preaching
became more precise, though as yet he was but a
Warner, with a mission to persuade, to promise rewards
and threaten punishments in the future, but with no
authority to compel men to accept his message. His
earliest converts after he went to the house of Arqam
were slaves, and these were by the hostile Meccans
subjected to torture by thirst and exposure in the
burning sands. Some recanted, but only for a time,
and were granted a special dispensation; but Bilāl, the
Abyssinian, endured every extreme without flinching.
In the fifth year of the preaching, Muhammad exhorted
his followers to seek refuge with the Najāshi (or King)

of Abyssinia, and thither many of them went, and were hospitably received : this is the first migration.

Considering the later antagonism between Christianity and the new religion, Islām, founded by Muhammad, and the harsh measures which he himself and, still more, his chief lieutenants took with Christian tribes and princes within a few years of this time, it seems strange that he should have sent his followers to take refuge at the court of the Christian King of Abyssinia. They and he, however, had every reason to be thankful for the choice, for they found a peaceful retreat with an honourable host. The fact will appear even more noteworthy when we remember that the Prophet was born in that same "year of the Elephant," when the hosts of Abyssinia advanced to the walls of Mecca. Muslim tradition has given us a fabulous account of what took place at the Court of the Najāshi ("Negus," as we know the title), between the refugees and the ambassadors from the Quraish, who demanded that they should be sent back to be dealt with in their own city. The story is apocryphal, no doubt, but it probably represents accurately enough the attitude of the king, and the doctrines at that time preached by the Reformer.

The two envoys of the Quraish had brought with them valuable gifts for the king and his courtiers, and had so won the ear of some of the chiefs. The king, however, resolved to hear both sides, and held an audience for the purpose. The envoys claimed to have the refugees expelled from Abyssinia and made over to them, on the ground that their leader had cast off the religion of his country, and was preaching another, " different alike from ours and from that of the King."

When they were introduced to the presence, the Quraish envoys prostrated themselves, as the custom of the country was, but the Muslims did not so, and boldly said, " By our Prophet's command we prostrate ourselves only before the One True God." The king wondered and was awed, and told them of the Quraish demand. At their request the king asked the envoys whether they were fugitive slaves, or claimed for debt, or for murder that lay on their heads, that they should be given up. But they answered, " Nay, they are free men and noble, neither are they fugitives for debt nor for blood ; but we claim them for the following reason : These people, O King, have abjured the religion of us and our forefathers; they have insulted, and are insulting, our gods, that they may corrupt the morals of our young men,—and so our harmony has been turned into discord. Give them up to us, that the old order of things may be restored."

Then, at the King's bidding, the Muslims declared how indeed they had followed the old idolatry till it pleased Allāh to send them His message through His apostle, a man of noble birth and blameless life, " who has shown us (they said) by infallible signs, proof of his mission, and has taught us to cast away idols and to worship the only true God. He has commanded us to abstain from all sin, to keep faith, to observe the times of fasting and of prayer, to love our kinsmen, to pay tithes, to purify our lives, and to follow after all virtue. Therefore do our enemies persecute us, and therefore have we, by our Prophet's command, sought refuge and protection in the King's country."

And when the King desired them to recite some part of their Prophet's wondrous message, they recited the first part of the chapter of *Mary*, wherein is told the story of the birth both of John the Baptist and of Jesus Christ, down to the account of Mary being fed with miraculous food. Thereupon the King and his bishops were affected to tears, and said it was even as in their gospel; and the King bade the envoys begone, for they should in no wise succeed.

Yet they tried again, urging that Muhammad and his followers blasphemed the Lord Jesus Christ. Again the Muslims were summoned, and asked what they thought of Jesus, and they answered, "Allah Most High hath said,[1]—He is the servant of God and His apostle, His word breathed into the Virgin's womb, a spirit from Him." And the King said, "Even so do we believe. Blessed be ye, and blessed is your master. I know him for the Prophet of God, foretold in the gospel. For no bribe will I give you up. Even as God gave me my land freely, so will I take no bribe." Then he returned to the Quraish their gifts, and sent them away; but the Muslims abode in his land unharmed.

The exiles, however, had not been very long in Abyssinia when they heard a report that the Prophet and the Quraish were reconciled, and returned homewards on the strength of it: and this indeed had happened for a short time. The story is a strange one, and has by many of the chief Muhammadan writers been suppressed or denied as dishonouring to the Prophet.

Muhammad, oppressed by a sense of failure in his mission, feeling how his efforts to turn his countrymen from their idols to the worship of the living and true God had all been powerless, was one day preaching at

[1] See Q. iv. 169–170.

the Kaaba, where were gathered the chiefs of the
Quraish, and recited the lofty claim to inspiration
(Sura 53),—"By the star when it falleth, your companion
erreth not, neither is he misled! nor speaketh he from
lust! It is but an inspiration breathed into him! One
taught him, who is mighty in power and of great understanding, appearing in the loftiest sphere.

" Then drew he near and hovered, till he was two bows'
length off or nigher still! Then he inspired his servant
with what he inspired him; the heart belies not what it
saw! What, will ye dispute with him on what he saw?

"Again, another time, he saw him (Gabriel) by the
Lote-tree which none may pass, near which is the
paradise of rest! When the Lote-tree covered its
mysteries, his sight turned not aside, nor did it
wander: he saw then the greatest of the signs of
his Lord.

"Have ye considered Al Lāt and Al Uzzā, and Manāt
the third with them?"

And then he yielded to the temptation of Satan, as
he afterwards said, or to the deceit of his own heart,
and he added—

"These are the high-soaring Cranes,[1] and verily their
intercession may be hoped for."

This was just the attitude of the idolaters, who held
them for daughters of God, who would intercede for
their worshippers. So, when the chapter was ended
with the words, " Wherefore bow down before God, and
serve Him!" the chiefs, gladly accepting the concession,
fell on their faces in adoration. They were satisfied to
admit Muhammud's claim to be the inspired Prophet of
God, if he would grant the divine intercessory powers of

[1] Or "swan-necked goddesses"; the word is not met with elsewhere.

their goddesses. And so peace was made, the news was swiftly carried to the exiles, and they returned to their homes.

But Muhammad was not long in seeing and repenting of his error and unfaithfulness. Muslim tradition makes his recovery almost immediate, averring that he retracted his error the very next day. That is not likely, but it was not long delayed. Instinctively he felt that everything was lost if he admitted partners with God, or acknowledged that the idols of Mecca were anything; and when next he came before his brethren, he substituted for the words of compromise an indignant denial of any power in the idols,—and so it stands to this day recorded—

"Shall there be male offspring unto you, and female unto Him? That were an unfair division! They are but names which ye have named, ye and your fathers! God has sent down no authority for them! They do but follow fancy and what their souls lust after!—And yet there has come to them guidance from their Lord. . . . How many an angel is in heaven! their intercession avails not at all, save after God has given permission." The truce was at an end, and Muhammad had finally broken with the idolaters. He had regained his lost position, and comforted himself and reassured his followers by ascribing the lapse to a passing temptation of the devil. But the exiles had returned, and the persecution began anew.

Muhammad himself was safe under the protection of his uncle Abu Tālib, who tried, indeed, once to persuade his nephew to abandon his new doctrine, but stood forth his protector none the less firmly when he refused, saying, " Though the sun should fight against me on my right hand and the moon on my left, yet shall I not hold back, till the Lord make manifest my cause, or I perish!" And when one day Muhammad could not be found, and there was fear of foul play, Abu Tālib gathered an armed band, prepared to take signal vengeance if his nephew had been murdered.

The exiles returning from Abyssinia found persecution hotter than ever, and soon after went back there,— and were followed at intervals by other converts, up to a total number of 101 adults, besides children (83 men and 18 women). Of these about 40 afterwards returned to Mecca, but the rest remained until they joined Muhammad at Medīna many years later. The Quraish again sent two envoys with rich gifts to the Najāshi, to try to get him to give up the fugitives; but after an audience they were sent back with a refusal. Muslim historians record that, though secretly for fear of his people, the King even embraced their doctrines— especially that which degrades the Saviour to the position of a mere Prophet; they say also that Muhammad on that ground offered up prayer for him after his death.

Meanwhile, at Mecca, Hamza, Muhammad's uncle and his foster-brother, the son of Abd al Muttalib's old age, afterwards surnamed the Lion of Islām, had joined the new faith, being roused at the persecution of his kinsman. An even more important adherent was Omar, son of Khattāb, afterwards second Khalifa, a man of dauntless courage and resolution, feared and respected in Mecca, and hitherto a bitter opponent of the new religion. The story runs that he had set out to murder Muhammad, but was arrested by the news that his own sister and brother-in-law were secret converts; he went to their house, abused and

assaulted them, but was himself converted by reading
the great Chapter "T. H.," the 20th of the Qurān,
which his sister gave him to read after he had
purified himself. "For none," said she, "save the pure
may look upon it." He then hastened to Muhammad
at the house of Arqam, and made public profession
of the Faith. The adhesion of these two powerful
citizens was of great moment; and Muhammad
waxed bold in his preaching; the number of his
followers increased; and the Quraish in alarm placed
the whole sect under interdict, by a formal deed,
registered and laid up in the Kaaba. For three
years it remained in force, during which time the
persecuted sect were shut up in the Shi'b, or Quarter,
of Hāshim, and were reduced to great extremity,—
being able to issue forth only during the sacred
months. At last the compassionate intervention of
some, led by the aged Abu Tālib, prevailed, and the
interdict was annulled, it being found that the writing
itself had been destroyed by white ants.

But the year of his release from the ban, the tenth
of his preaching (620 A.D.), brought Muhammad the
heaviest sorrows of his life, for within a few months he
was bereaved of his faithful wife Khadīja and of his
lifelong protector Abu Tālib. The place of the latter
as a protector was taken for a time by his uncle Abu
Lahb, who soon cast him off again on finding out that he
condemned to hell all their common ancestry. Khadīja's
place was filled up by a marriage with Sauda, now a
widow returned from Abyssinia, whose first husband
Sakrān had lately died in Mecca, and by a betrothal to
Ayesha, daughter of Abu Bakr, now only six years old,
—the marriage taking place at Medīna three years later.

As all the glowing pictures of sensual delights in paradise had by this time been "revealed," and as Khadīja was sixty-five years old at her death, it is not unfair to suggest that Muhammad was now yielding to passions which had hitherto been repressed, and to which in his after life he gave free rein, with effects ruinous to the moral teaching of his religion.

The death of Khadīja, closely followed by that of Abu Tālib, together with the forced exile of his followers to Abyssinia and renewed persecution by his fellow-citizens, compelled Muhammad to look elsewhere for a field favourable for his mission. He first sought converts in the neighbouring town of fertile Tā,if, but was driven away with insult and pelted with stones, and returned sad at heart to Mecca, with his one faithful attendant Zaid. In after days he told in the Qurān how Jinns in the valley of Nakhla had hearkened to the message which men had rejected. There remained only the hope of success with strangers, since he had so little honour in his own country, and to them, but especially to his kinsfolk in Medīna, Muhammad now turned his hopes. The annual pilgrimage brought opportunity, of which he was quick to avail himself. Just as Qās of Najrān had fired his own boyish spirit in earlier years, so did he seek to move those who now came to the Feasts. Medīna too was ripe for his purpose; the mutual rivalry of the Aus and Khazraj, and that of both with the strong Jewish element, made the situation favourable for Muhammad. Neither of the three parties could well have brooked the supremacy of one of the others, and a stranger of commanding ability and character might well aspire to rule the city. Tradition further records that the Arabs of Medīna, "polytheists and idolaters," had been threatened by the Jews with the speedy advent of a Prophet, under whom they should be smitten even as the children of Ad and Iram had been. And, says the teller of the tale, " we had grace from God to listen to His Messenger when he came, but the Jews (though they knew him) hardened their hearts : and therefore they were slain."

During the year 620, Muhammad was in much anxiety as to what turn matters would take in Medīna, and whether his handful of converts there would prove faithful. If not, his chances of success in Arabia would be lost for ever, and he himself forced to exile beyond its borders. But with the pilgrimage of 621 A.D., his fears were dispelled by the appearance of twelve men, ten of Khazraj and two of Aus, whom he met in a sheltered glen of Minā. They avowed their faith in Muhammad, and swore : " We will not worship any but the One God ; we will not steal, neither will we commit adultery, nor kill our children ; we will not slander in any wise ; and we will not disobey the Prophet in anything that is right." This is the Pledge of Women, so called because there was no promise to fight for the Prophet or the faith. And Muhammad answered them : " If ye fulfil the pledge, paradise shall be your reward. He that shall fail in ought thereof, to God it belongeth to punish him or forgive." The oath is known also as the First Pledge of Aqaba, the little terraced mound where it was given. The twelve returned to Medīna ; the doctrine was zealously preached from house to house with wonderful success, and in the course of the year Muhammad, at his converts' desire, sent, to reinforce them, Musāb, one of the returned

exiles of Abyssinia, who was "mighty in the Qurān,"
—probable though not conclusive evidence that much
of the "revelation" had by that time been committed
to writing.

During the year 621–622 A.D., as Muir well remarks,
the revelations grow in firmness, and breathe a defiant
and aggressive spirit. Muhammad felt that his time
of power was approaching, that the days of unequal
struggle against the powers of Mecca were nearly at
an end, and he poured out warning, threats, and scorn.
His faith was justified; for when the pilgrimage
season again came round, he met the converts of
Medīna once more at Aqaba, not now twelve men only,
but seventy-five,—who pledged their faith to him in
the presence of his uncle Abbās, who (though himself
still an idolater) adjured them not to draw his nephew
away from the safeguard of his own kindred unless
prepared to defend him to the death. Then in the
stillness of night, in low, hurried conference for fear
of their watchful foes, hands of fealty were grasped,
and the men of Medīna swore to defend the Prophet as
they would their own wives and children. He blessed
their resolution, chose from among them twelve to be
his special men of trust, "by the inspiration of God,
through his angel Gabriel," and agreed shortly to
follow them to make his home in Medīna. Thus, on
the night of 31st March to 1st April, 622 A.D., when
was taken the Second Pledge of Aqaba, Muhammad
crossed his Rubicon, and prepared to follow his mighty
career in Medīna. Silently, as they had come, his
followers stole away to rejoin the main body of
pilgrims, the inquiries of the suspicious Quraish
were skilfully baffled, and the divine command to

emigrate went forth. The men of Medīna got back
to their homes, and the Faithful from Mecca gradually
followed them, till of the men there remained behind
only Ali, Abu Bakr, and the Prophet himself.

The Quraish were puzzled and alarmed, and at last
they resolved in common council to assassinate the
Prophet, one murderer being chosen from each tribe,
that so his own kinsmen might be compelled to accept
the bloodwit. This proposal is said to have been made
by a strange sheikh, really Satan in human form,
and (naturally) Muhammad was warned of the plot
by the angel Gabriel. Abu Bakr had brought two
fine riding-camels for himself and the Prophet, and
had brought them into perfect condition; and one
evening they started on their momentous journey,
gallant Ali staying behind, wrapped in Muhammad's
well-known mantle, and lying on his bed in Abu
Tālib's house to deceive the Quraish. The stratagem
succeeded, and the intending murderers went away
baffled. Muhammad and Abu Bakr left Mecca on the
evening of Monday, 21st June 622, and for some days
lay concealed in the cave of Tora. Food and intelli-
gence was brought them secretly from Mecca, while
Quraish scouts scoured the country to take them, and
earn the price offered for their capture. But the
seekers were foiled. Tradition loved to tell how doves
(henceforward safe from every true Muslim) built their
nests, and spiders wove their webs before the cave ; how
a tree miraculously sprang up at its mouth ; and how,
when an eager, well-armed pursuer did overtake the
fugitives, his camel sank deep into the sand until he
swore not to betray them. It is even told that Gabriel
appeared as a man, and *lied* to a band of Quraish to

6

save the Prophet. But one fine trait is probably
historical, that when even Abu Bakr trembled at the
peril to "them two left alone," Muhammad cheered
him with the assurance that the Almighty was with
them, "the third." As soon as the danger was past,
the two fugitives made their way by stages, as rapid
as was consistent with safety, to Medīna. They
reached the village of Qubā, in its neighbourhood, in
about ten days, were there heartily welcomed, and
entered the city itself probably on Monday, 28th June
622. This was the Hijra ("Hegira"), the Flight, and
henceforward Muhammad the Prophet of Allah became a temporal prince also, commissioned to add
force to persuasion in extending Islām. For nearly
eleven years he ruled with a sway most absolute over
an ever-increasing nation, and at his death he left his
empire vigorous and firmly established to the capable
fostering hands of Abu Bakr.

The last days in Mecca are marked by a wonderful
vision of the night, transformed by tradition ascribed
to Muhammad himself into an actual miraculous journey from Mecca to "the further temple" at Jerusalem,
and an ascent through the circles of heaven and the
companies of adoring prophets and angels into the
immediate presence of God Almighty, far beyond where
even Gabriel could ascend. There he received from
God Himself the command for the five daily prayers
incumbent on every Muslim, there he saw the
"wonders of his Lord," and a vision of the destinies
of men. The Christian will at once be reminded of St.
Paul's mysterious rapture, and the tale of the gradual
lightening of the burden of daily prayers from fifty to
five will recall Abraham pleading for Sodom; but he

will wonder and grieve at the blasphemy which places
his Lord only in the second heaven, far beneath
Abraham, Moses, and others. Muslim doctors are
divided as to whether this journey was material, or
only spiritual, the reference to it in the Qurān itself is
brief and obscure (Chap. xvii. 1); but the great mass
of the "faithful" believe every word of the marvellous
story in its most literal sense.

The words of the Qurān which refer to the
wonderful journey, be it in the spirit only or in the
body, are these: "Celebrated be the praises of Him
who took His servant a journey by night from the
Sacred Mosque (the Kaaba at Mecca) to the Remote
Mosque (the Temple at Jerusalem), the precinct of
which We have blessed, to show him of our signs!
verily, He both hears and looks." [1] The event accordingly is known as either the Night Journey (Isrā), or
the Ascension (Miraj), the latter referring to the successive stages by which the Prophet mounts through
the seven heavens to pass into the immediate presence
of God, far beyond the limit to which even Gabriel was
allowed to soar. The account of the journey comes
from the Prophet's own lips, by a chain of faithful
witnesses, and its truth was expressly vouched for by
trusty Abu Bakr. It is one, the greatest, of the three
miraculous events in the Prophet's life,—the others being
the "splitting of the moon in twain," said to have been
vouchsafed as a sign to the unbelievers of Mecca, and
the legion of angel auxiliaries that came to help the
little Muslim host at the battle of Badr.

As he slept at night in the house of Umm Hāni,
sister of Ali, he was roused by Gabriel, with whom was

[1] Palmer.

the Archangel Michael. Again, as once before in his childhood, they opened his breast, washed his heart in water from the holy well Zemzem, and filled it with Faith and Wisdom. They then mounted him on a mysterious animal that with lightning speed transported him to the rock at Jerusalem on which the Temple stood, and where to this day is shown the ring to which he fastened it, and the mark of his blessed foot as he alighted. But as he passed on his wonderful way, the angel pointed out Medīna as his future abode, and bade him pray as he went by; he also resisted, through divine aid, the allurements of the world (presented in the shape of a beautiful woman), and of Jewish and Christian doctrine, figured in the guise of a bowl of wine and a cup of water. On arrival at the temple rock, he was reverently welcomed by a throng of angels and prophets; and as it was the time of midnight prayer, he led the devotions of the august assembly. They hailed him as " First, and last, and assembler!"—first, as Gabriel interpreted, to be raised after death from paradise to heaven, first to be permitted to intercede with God for mankind; last of the prophets sent by God to men; and leader on the Judgment-day of those who shall find mercy! Then began the ascent through the circles of heaven to the threshold of which he was borne on the wings of the Archangel.

At the portal of the first heaven the angel knocked, and a voice from within inquired who sought admittance. Gabriel answered, "It is I, Gabriel," But again the voice asked, "Is there any with thee?" and he said, "Muhammad." Again came the question, "Hath he been called (to the office of prophet)?" and

he answered, " Yes." Then was the gate opened, and
they entered; and Adam greeted Muhammad with the
words, "Welcome, pious son and pious Prophet!"
Then Muhammad beheld, and saw two doors, the one
on Adam's right hand, and the other on his left. As
oft as he looked towards the first he laughed with
delight, and there issued therefrom a sweet savour; but
as often as he turned to the other he wept, and from it
came evil odours; and the Prophet marvelled, and
asked of Gabriel what this should mean; and it was
told him that the one door led to Paradise, and the
other to Hell, and that the Father of mankind rejoiced
over those who were saved, and wept over those of his
children who were lost. Then they soared upward to
the second heaven, to which they entered after the
same questions and answers as at the first; and there
were two young men, John the Baptist and Jesus; and
they greeted Muhammad, " Welcome, pious brother and
pious Prophet!" Thence they passed to the third
heaven, to receive the same welcome from Joseph,
" whose beauty excelled that of all other creatures as
far as the light of the full moon surpasses that of the
stars"; then to the fourth, where Enoch greeted them;
and the fifth, where Aaron welcomed them with the
same words. In the sixth heaven, Moses welcomed
him as his brother and a Prophet; but he wept as he
soared above him,—not for envy of Muhammad's glory
surpassing his own, but to think that so few of his
own nation were appointed to Paradise. From the
heaven of Moses, the Archangel led Muhammad up to
the seventh, where he showed him Abraham, "his
Father," who bade him, " Welcome, pious son and pious
Prophet!" In this seventh heaven the Prophet beheld

the wondrous Tree, the abode of Gabriel, round which
fly countless myriads of angels; from its foot spring
the two rivers of Paradise, and the two great rivers of
earth—Euphrates and the Nile; and "the light of God
overspreads the whole Tree." There too was the
heavenly Kaaba, the original of the Meccan, and
round it went, in adoring circuit, radiant armies of
angels; so vast indeed is their number that the same
worshipping host never returns after once making the
mystic round!

Beyond the seventh heaven Gabriel could only go
with the Prophet, and that by special permission, as far
as the first of the seventy veils of dazzling light (each five
hundred years' journey from the next!) that shut in the
Throne of God. As the Prophet passed each successive
stage, the gracious Voice bade him "Come nearer!" till
at last he entered the immediate presence of God.
There he was endowed with perfect wisdom and knowledge, cheered with the promise that all who received
his message should be taken into Paradise, and commanded to lay on his faithful followers the duty of
praying fifty times in the day. The Prophet returned
from God's Presence-Chamber to the lower heavens, and
told Moses of the duty laid upon him. But by the old
Lawgiver's advice he time after time ventured back to
plead with his Lord, till the burden of the daily
prayers was reduced to five—the perpetual ordinance
of Islām.

Then with lightning speed the Prophet was returned
to his chamber at Mecca, and, for all the wondrous
things he had seen, yet was the bed still warm when he
lay down again.[1]   And in the morning he went to the

[1] Scoffers of Akbar's court made merry over this!

Kaaba, and told the wondrous tale to a sceptical audience; and they plied him with questions as to the temple at Jerusalem, where by ordinary journey he never had been, and he returned true and convincing answers, " for the angel Gabriel held up before my eyes, as I spoke, a true model of the Holy Place."

This whole wonderful story deserves a place in every account of Muhammad, and has received it in most. It has been told in all the earliest Lives of the Prophet, and is embalmed in all collections of Traditions as a veritable record from his own lips. Pious fancy has no doubt embellished it, and many marvellous details have here been omitted; but all commentators attach the story to the words already quoted from the Qurān, and the mystical journey is as instructive for our view of Muhammad's character and teaching, whether it be meant as an allegory or to be taken as literally true. All the elements, no doubt, might be traced to rabbinical or apocryphal Christian sources, we may safely take it that the sublime glories of Moses " speaking face to face with God" on Mount Sinai, and of the Mount of Transfiguration, were present to Muhammad's mind; but it is to his own immense self-importance that we must charge the strange ordering of God's messengers and prophets, and his degrading of the Saviour of men—another mark of the Antichrist. Yet throughout there is poverty of imagination; all that is great and sublime is borrowed; and it is but a poor or perverted mind which would compare the story with the grandeurs and mysteries of the Apocalypse!

CHAPTER VII

Muhammad reaches Medīna—Religious and Political Institutions
—"Refugees" and "Helpers": Bond of Brotherhood—The
Jews—Attacks on Meccan Commerce—Battle of Badr: Its
Critical Importance—Treatment of the Captives—Joy in
Medīna—Reprisals against Foes in Medīna—Exile of Jews—
Marriage of Fātima to Ali—Defeat of Muhammad at Uhud—
The Prophet wounded—Khālid—Hamza slain—The Funeral
Hymn—Assassinations—Exile of more Jews.

THE first news of Muhammad's coming to Medīna was
given to his anxious disciples by a Jewish watcher,
who proclaimed the glad news on the evening of
Monday, 28th June 622 A.D. (eight days after the
exiles had left Mecca); for the Jews, said Muhammad
afterwards, "knew him better than their own
children." The news quickly spread, his adherents
hurried forth to welcome him and Abu Bakr, and
for a night or two he rested in Qubā, and then entered
Yathrib (as it then was),—Medīna, "the City," as it
has ever since been. In his entry he did not disdain
a little display quite in accordance with Arab modes
of thought; for when his followers would have stopped
his camel, the famous Al Qaswā, and made it kneel,
Muhammad checked them, and when the camel of her
own accord stopped, all accepted the choice as matter
of divine guidance, and possible jealousies were avoided.
This was Friday, 2nd July, and on his march from

Qubā, Muhammad held his first public service and preaching amid one hundred converts, and Friday was fixed as the day of public prayer for all Islām. Where the camel stopped was an open space, and that ground Muhammad purchased at its full value from two orphan lads; there he established his house, and hard by he built later the sacred Mosque of Medīna; and there his body was ten years later laid to its final rest.

Muhammad's power was spiritual first and temporal afterwards; he was the founder of a new religion before he became the head of a new earthly empire,—and accordingly he gave his care to the Church before the State; but political soon followed religious institutions. The Mosque was founded, the five daily prayers appointed, and Friday chosen for the weekly religious assembly, when all the faithful came together to follow the Prophet in prayer and to hear from his lips the words of exhortation. A special call to prayer was instituted,—that by the human voice, instead of by Jewish trumpet or Christian bell. The happy inspiration was due to Omar, and the weird music of the Muazzin's voice from myriads of minarets still floats in the air in all the countries of Islām, with unwearied call repeating: "God is most great! I witness that there is no god but God, and Muhammad is the Prophet of God! Come to prayer! come to salvation! God is most great! There is no god but God"; with the addition, at dawn,—"Prayer is better than sleep!" and for emphasis each phrase is twice or thrice repeated. These were the pillars of religious practice, to which were added later the month's fast in Ramadhān, and the solemn feasts, the *Qiblah* (direction to which the face should be turned when praying), and the Greater and Lesser Pilgrimage. But Muhammad, an Arab in every fibre of his being, knew well the strength and the weakness of his people's character, and set himself without delay to make use of both to build up and secure his power on the political side as well.

Envy is the curse of the Arab, and tribal jealousies had hitherto been fatal to Arab power. Muhammad, following an old custom, established " brotherhood " of the closest kind between his followers from Mecca and the converts of Medīna, one of each being made " brothers," a tie which was to supersede those of kindred, each even inheriting from the other,—which arrangement was not abrogated till after the battle of Badr two years later. This measure had the double result of preventing jealousy between " Refugees " (from Mecca) and "Helpers" (*Ansār*) of Medīna, but also of effacing that between Muslims of the rival tribes Aus and Khazraj, very lately at deadly feud. With the Jews, too, Muhammad made a treaty of close alliance, offensive and defensive. Each party was to keep its own religion without interference from the other, they were to have equal rights, and to fight to the uttermost for one another: it was added, " No believer shall be put to death for slaying an infidel, nor shall any infidel be upheld against a believer." All discordant elements were thus for the time united, and the Prophet's power grew apace. He now turned his thoughts to offensive operations against Mecca that had rejected him, and began welding his forces together for the great struggle which he had perhaps long meditated. That the strife was begun by

him is clear, for Mecca, relieved by his departure, took
no hostile steps, and allowed his family and those of
his followers to leave without molestation. It is easy
to understand how Hamza and Omar, Ali, Zaid, and
others, fiery Arabs all of them, would fall in with
plans of revenge, and how gladly they would hail the
prospect of at once punishing their former oppressors
and enriching themselves.

The commerce of Mecca depended on the half-yearly
caravans, of which the more important was that to
Syria, passing along the Red Sea shore northward at
no great distance from Medīna. Before the end of the
year of the Flight, a small party was sent out under
Hamza to cut off the caravan on its way north, but the
expedition failed. A second and a third band was sent
out, and to the leader of each Muhammad gave a white
standard ; the Prophet himself led two equally abortive
forays, to Abwā and Bairāt respectively ; but it was
not till November 623 A.D. that the first blood was
shed by Muslims in battle, when a small force under
Abdallah broke, at Nakhla, the truce of the sacred
month Rajab, rather than let their prey escape.
When the sacrilegious act was reported to Muhammad,
he, after some hesitation, declared the sanction of
heaven for the deed : "it is a less evil to break the
sacred truce than to expel God's Prophet" ; and
Paradise was promised to such as should die fighting
for the Faith. Thus, in the end of 623 A.D., was
promulgated the law of *Jihād* or Holy War, henceforward such a prominent feature of the new religion.

The sword once unsheathed was not long to remain
idle. The Syrian caravan had passed northward unharmed in the autumn, under the wary guidance of

Abu Sufiyān, but its return brought about the critical battle of Badr,—which is to Muslim history all and more than all that Hastings means in the history of England. The caravan was returning, and as usual every Meccan who could afford it had some share in the venture. Muhammad himself led out his forces to cut it off. The little army consisted of 300 men, it started from Medīna on Sunday, 12th Ramadhān, 8th January 624 A.D., and marched to Badr, two days out from Medīna. Hitherto the men of Medīna were pledged only to *defend* Muhammad, but now with one voice they vowed to aid him no less in attack, and the fusion of his followers was complete. Abu Sufiyān, having news of the attack intended, sent to Mecca an urgent appeal for help; and the citizens marched out, nearly a thousand strong, to his aid. But by skilful leading the caravan escaped its pursuers, and the relieving army hesitated whether to march on against Muhammad or to return. Strong appeals were made on both sides; great reluctance was shown to embitter the quarrel; but the voices of those prevailed whose kindred had already fallen, and the army set forward.

On Muhammad's side there was no feeling of compunction or regret. He knew the fiery courage of his followers, he counted perhaps on divided counsels among his foes, and he made ready with stern confidence for the struggle, himself setting the battle in order. On this, as on all occasions, he showed great qualities as a commander. He had the first of these in the magic power he exercised over his troops, their absolute and unquestioning faith in and devotion to him. The field of battle is a plain, with steep hills on the north and east, and contained several wells of water. Acting on friendly advice, Muhammad seized the most advanced of these, which was also the best, and destroyed the others. This was a great advantage, and the Quraish suffered much loss in their attempts to get water. Night fell, and the Prophet's army enjoyed quiet rest, while he was cheered in his sleep by visions of success ; but the enemy were dismayed by portents and prophecies of evil. When morning broke the forces of Islām were arrayed for battle, with its three white standards displayed, and their foes advanced to the attack. But the latter, marching from the west, were dazzled by the rising sun, and moved heavily over sand that had been sodden by rain. The great superiority in numbers, however, made the position critical, and Muhammad retired to strengthen himself with fervent prayer, pleading with God to fight with him against the idolaters, and not to suffer His truth to be overborne; and stout Abu Bakr strengthened his heart with assurance that his prayer would be heard.

The Quraish attacked,—but the general engagement was preceded by several single combats. Hamza, Ali, and Ubaida, especially distinguished themselves, and carried the omen of victory for their side. Muhammad probably did only his part as commander, though there is no ground for charging him (as Sprenger does) with personal cowardice ; while the spirit he infused into his men is witnessed by the fiery valour of Umair, a lad of sixteen, who flung away some dates he was eating, crying out, " these keep me back from Paradise," cast himself into the foemen's ranks, and died bravely fighting.

It was a stormy winter day, and Muhammad transformed the fierce blasts that swept across the valley into a legion of angels under Gabriel and Michael, fighting for the believers, — as the "great Twin Brethren" had fought for Rome at Lake Regillus! Stories were told of how they had even made prisoners for the Muslims. The battle raged fiercely, but at last the fiery valour of the Muslims prevailed; as the foe wavered, Muhammad stooped, threw a handful of pebbles towards them, and cried, "Confusion seize their faces!" They turned to flee, defeat was turned to rout; the Quraish cast away their arms, and abandoned their camp and baggage; and Muhammad had won his first great victory. Of his men only fourteen had fallen, of whom eight were Refugees; the Quraish lost forty-nine killed, and a like number wounded. Among the slain were many of the chief men of Mecca, and Muhammad showed fierce exultation when there was brought to him the head of his bitter foe, his uncle, Abu Jahl.

Some few of the prisoners were slain in cold blood, but the majority were held to ransom. Each man was allowed to retain the spoil of any he had himself slain; but the general booty was divided on the principle that one-fifth should be at the Prophet's disposal for personal and public purposes, and the remainder divided among the troops,—all sharing equally, whether they had fought in the front of battle or had stayed to guard the camp. In this matter also Jewish precedent was followed. The enemy's dead were buried in a trench on the field, and as they were cast into the common grave, Muhammad addressed the chief by name: "Have ye now found the promise of your Lord to come true? Woe to you, who rejected me, your Prophet! Verily, my Lord's promise to me hath been

made good!" And he told his wondering followers
that truly the dead heard his words.

Then he returned to Medīna; poured into mourning
hearts the balm of comfortable words; yet on the way
he gratified private revenge by ordering two of his
captives, Nadhr and Uqba, to be put to death. The
fierce spirit of Islām is shown by the reply of the
captor to an appeal for mercy, "Islām has severed all
bonds"; and Muhammad himself answered Uqba, who
pleaded for his little daughter, "Hell-fire will care
for her!"

The Quraish went back in mourning to Mecca, but
their fierce spirit for long refused to wail for the dead
that had fallen, or to seek to ransom the captives.
The women were specially bitter, and stirred the men
to revenge,—which was taken amply in the following
year at Uhud; but the moral effect of the victory at
Badr was never effaced, and from it dates Muhammad's
triumphant career. The captives that were spared
were well and generously treated; those who could
not pay a money-ransom were allowed to redeem
themselves by teaching boys of Medīna to write;
several embraced Islām, and the well-judged clemency
greatly advanced the cause of the new Faith. But
this mercy was mainly due to the mild counsels of
Abu Bakr, for Muhammad had published the "revelation" (Q. viii. 70), "It is not for the Prophet to take
prisoners, or to accept ransom: it is at his choice to
slay them if he will."

The news of the great victory was carried by Zaid
to Medīna, and the very children triumphed over the
death of Abu Jahl. To Muhammad, however, the joy
of victory was dimmed by the news which met him

on his return, of the death, during his absence, of his
daughter Rukāya, wife of Uthmān.

Freed by the defeat of the Meccan army from foreign
attack, Muhammad set himself to remove from his
path stumbling-blocks in Medīna.   Chief among these
were the strong Jewish tribes, who formed (as they
have ever done) a nationality apart.   The causes of
strife lay on the surface; each party was bitterly
disappointed with the other; Muhammad had hoped
to be accepted by the Jews as the great Prophet, the
Messiah foretold in their law,—and the Jews hoped,
from his declared aim to " restore the religion of
Abraham," that he would join their faith and serve
their ambition.   Neither would yield : the Jews would
own no prophet that came not of Abraham's seed, and
Muhammad would not subordinate his claims to any.
He proceeded therefore to open war.

The first victim was a woman, a poetess, Asmā,
daughter of Marwān.   She was an idolater, and had
roused Muhammad's hatred by verses attacking him
and denouncing her people's folly for trusting him.   A
blind man, Umair, with Muhammad's knowledge,
stabbed her to death at night with every circumstance
of savagery, and the Prophet blessed him for the
service at public prayer next day.   The next victim
was an aged Jew proselyte, also guilty of writing
poetry against Muhammad : he too was foully murdered,—and terror spread among the " Disaffected."

These two murders were followed by a regular attack
on one of the three Jewish tribes, the Qainuqāa.   It
was alleged against the Jews generally that they
strove, covertly to sow dissension among the Muslims,
but the special pretext for the attack was insult in

their bāzār (they were goldsmiths) to a Muslim girl, in revenge for which a Jew was slain, and his murderer in retaliation. By treaty Muhammad was bound to judicial inquiry; but instead he went forth with a strong following to the Jewish settlement, angrily summoned them to submit to him as their Prophet, and, on their refusal, raised the great white banner, and laid siege to them. After fifteen days of close investment, no help from any quarter appearing, they surrendered at discretion, and were led forth bound for execution. The strong remonstrance of Abdallah, son of Ubai, the Khazraj chief, whom Muhammad dared not refuse, prevailed to save them from death. They were pitilessly driven into exile, and found their way with much hardship to a new home among their kinsfolk in Syria; their lands and wealth fell to the conqueror; and another instance was given that "Islām had broken all ties."

The following months were only disturbed by minor expeditions by and against the Quraish. Abu Sufiyān made a successful foray, and Zaid retaliated by cutting off and plundering at Karada, in Najd, a rich Meccan caravan. But before the third year after the Flight closed, Muhammad once more stained his fame by a peculiarly treacherous murder, again of a Jew and a poet, Ashraf, son of Kāb,—whose death he compassed by means of his own foster-brother. The murderer fiercely retorted, when challenged by his own brother, that he would slay *him* if the Prophet bade him; and, says the story, the brother and all his house embraced Islām!

The year closed with the Prophet taking a third wife, Hafsa, daughter of Omar, and giving in marriage

7

to Ali his daughter Fātima, from which union descends the numerous stock of the Sayyids, the nobility of Islām. None was more worthy than Ali, brave, generous, devoted; yet in his character was a strain of weakness and indecision that was to prove disastrous to himself, and fatal also to his sons, Hasan and Husain, the martyred Imāms, objects of the idolatrous veneration of the great Schism. By his own marriage to Hafsa, Muhammad allied himself as closely to Omar as he already was to Abu Bakr; there continued rivalry between the two wives, but Ayesha's position was never seriously in danger but once.

In the following year (A.H. 3), just a twelvemonth after the victory of Badr, Muhammad met with a severe defeat at Uhud. The Quraish had ever since their disaster at Badr been making ready to avenge it. The profits of the escaped caravan had been by unanimous vote of the citizens devoted to equipping a new army, and in the beginning of 625 A.D. a large force of Meccans and their allies (3000 men, of whom 700 were mail-clad warriors) set out for Medīna. Muhammad's uncle, Abbās, contrived to send him timely warning of the threatened attack, and every possible effort was made to meet it. The chief women of Mecca, fiercer even than the men, went with the troops, and Hind, wife of Abu Sufiyān, is infamous in Muslim history for her savage thirst for vengeance against Hamza. The invaders encamped, after ten days' march, in the rich plain of Uhud, five miles from Medīna, from which they were separated by some rocky ridges, and ravaged the country round, destroying crops and fruit-trees, with the object of drawing the enemy into the open and overwhelming them.

The public assembly was convened in the Mosque, and an informal council of war held. Muhammad advised, and Abdallah ibn Ubai agreed, that the women and children should be brought from the villages within the city walls, and the enemy left to exhaust themselves without risking a battle. But the rasher counsels of more fiery spirits prevailed; Muhammad yielded, delivered a stirring address to his followers, gave the sacred banners, and himself led forth the host. As he advanced he saw Abdallah's Jewish allies coming up, and ordered them back, "for ye shall not seek help of idolaters against idolaters." In view of subsequent events this story may well be an invention.

The battle was fought on Saturday, 11th January, and the odds against Muhammad, already very great, were much increased by the desertion of Abdallah with his 300 men,—leaving only 700 to face four times their number. Though the enemy was full in sight, the usual morning prayer was offered, and then the Prophet again showed his skill as a general. He drew up his little army with their rear protected by the steep rocks of Uhud, and guarded a gap by which he might be outflanked with a picked body of archers,— to whom he gave positive orders to hold the position whatever the course of the main engagement; he then awaited the attack. The first to fall was Talha, who bore the Quraish standard, slain by Ali; Muhammad cried aloud, "Great is the Lord!"[1] and the whole army took up the shout of triumph. Uthmān caught the standard from his dying brother's hand, while women clashed their timbrels and sang songs of encouragement, but he too fell beneath the sword of Hamza;

[1] *Allāhu Akbar*, the Takbīr.

nor did the deadly fight for the standard cease till the whole family of Talha, two brothers and three sons, were laid low.

Then the battle became general. Ali, Hamza, Dujāna, —armed with a sword by Muhammad himself,— Zubair, and others, conspicuous by ostrich plume or gay feather, did mighty deeds of valour ; the archer-band kept the Meccan horse at bay ; and it seemed as if the smaller force might even win the fight. But the advantage was too eagerly pressed, a party fell to plundering ere the victory was secure, the flanking body of archers joined in the premature pillage, Khālid, the great Meccan general (afterwards a tower of strength to Islām), swooped down with his cavalry on Muhammad's left and rear, and the army of the Prophet was put to rout. Then fell Musāb, who bore his standard ; gallant Hamza was thrust through with a javelin ; and Muhammad himself was badly wounded in the face. He tried in vain to stem the flight, and owed his life to the valour and devotion of a handful of his followers. Stunned and wounded he was hurried to a place of safety, where the remnant of his army gathered round him. The rumour that he was slain spread dismay among his followers, and his foes triumphed. Fortunately the false report caused the pursuit to slacken, while the field was searched for the Prophet's body ; meanwhile the wound was dressed, and Muhammad solemnly cursed his sacrilegious foes. A boastful challenge by Abu Sufiyān, answered by Omar, showed that Muhammad, Abu Bakr, and he still lived ; the Quraish chief's shout of triumph was met by a fervent cry of confidence in God ; and the Meccan army withdrew, making a tryst for a second battle at Badr a year later. Seventy-four of Muhammad's men lay dead upon the field, among them gallant Hamza, whose dead body Hind, wife of Abu Sufiyān, savagely mutilated, and the brave standard-bearer, Musāb; but the enemy had lost twenty only.

Medīna was a city of mourning when the news came. The women hurried forth to tend the wounded and to weep for the dead; the malcontents spoke hard things of Muhammad, and the faith of his followers was sorely tried by the defeat. But he rose against the tide of reproach, pronounced blessings over the martyrs who had died for their faith, and chiefly over Hamza, " the Lion of God and the Lion of His Apostle," now in bliss in the highest Paradise. He encouraged his followers at the weekly prayer with some of the finest and most impassioned utterances to be found in the Qurān :—

" We will surely cast terror into the hearts of the infidels, for presumptuously joining others with God ! Their resting-place shall be the fire,—a woeful abode for transgressors !

" And some of you chose the present life, and some the life to come; and He caused you to flee before your foes, that He might prove you !

" Think not at all that they are dead, who were slain in the way of the Lord. Nay, they live in the presence of their Lord, rejoicing in His bounty, and for those who shall follow in their steps. No terror afflicts them, neither are they grieved."

And in reference to his own reported death, he uttered the solemn words, forgotten (it would seem), when he was taken from his people, till Abu Bakr recalled them :—

" Muhammad is no more than an apostle, as other

apostles that have gone before him. What! if he should die or be killed, must ye needs turn back upon your heels? He that turneth back in no wise injureth God; but God will reward the thankful."

With such words did Muhammad cheer and bind up the hearts of his followers, as they hung upon his lips, while he spoke leaning on the palm-tree pillar in the great Mosque. Their faith in him was absolute, and the spirit of martyrdom was theirs, wherewith to crush down every doubt and fear, to triumph even in seeming defeat. But, as Muhammad had shown himself a bold and skilful commander in the field, so now as soon as the first outburst of grief was past, he gathered a handful of troops and hung on the rear of his victorious foes. He even captured and put to death two of those who fought against him, one of whom had already once been his prisoner, and whom he sentenced with the stern words, "Verily thou shall not say, I deceived the Prophet *twice*." It was after the battle of Uhud that Muhammad promulgated the important law under which a widow and daughter succeed, in the absence of male issue, to the family inheritance, a brother taking only a small share instead of (as formerly) the whole. The Christian reader will recall the decree of Moses in the case of the daughters of Zelophehad.

The victory of Uhud, though the Meccans did not follow it up, encouraged other foes. Within a few months Muhammad defeated the Bani Asad, a powerful tribe in Najd, from whom he took rich booty, and forestalled the attack by the Bani Lahyān by procuring the assassination of their chief. The assassin was not only sent out by Muhammad, but was specially blessed by him when he returned with his victim's head. Such acts provoked retaliation, and not long after six Muslims were overpowered while on a peaceful mission, and two of them cruelly put to death. They died bravely, but not without bitterly cursing their murderers, and tradition tells that the curse was fulfilled to the letter. In the same year (A.H. 4) a much larger party, forty or seventy men, were treacherously murdered by another tribe of Najd, the Bani Amir; and in retaliation, two of the tribe, returning from Medīna under a safe conduct, were murdered,—and for them Muhammad honourably paid the bloodwit. But for his own, foully slain, he bitterly cursed the treacherous clans and all their kindred, and brought as from the dead themselves a message: "Say to our people that we have met our Lord. He with us is well pleased, and we with Him."

But the tale of bloodshed was not complete. The Bani Amir were confederate with the Jewish tribe of Nazīr, and to them the Prophet applied for help in the blood-money. But ere a reply could be given he abruptly departed, and sent his command that they should go into exile. Abdallah ibn Ubai tried in vain to heal the quarrel, and then the Jews, hoping for help from him, determined on resistance; but after a siege which lasted three weeks, they were forced to surrender, when Muhammad, contrary to the usages of Arab warfare, had destroyed their date-trees and ravaged their lands. They then, like their brethren the Qainuqāa, went forth into exile, and the spoil fell to their conqueror. Thus had two of the great Jewish tribes been driven into exile; the third, the Bani Quraiza, which had shrunk from their help, was reserved for a worse fate, nor was it long before that fate overtook them.

Again Muhammad raised an exulting pæan in his revelation, and forged, under the sanction of his Lord, new weapons of attack, and new threatenings for his foes.

The breach with the Jews was now complete, and Muhammad could no longer, as before, trust a Jew secretary. He therefore chose one of his own followers for the office, Zaid, son of Thābit, and this choice was momentous, for it is to this Zaid that we owe the collection of the Qurān, the ultimate basis of almost all our knowledge of Muhammad, and of which we are "as sure that it is the word of the Prophet, as his followers are that it is the word of God."

CHAPTER VIII

Muhammad's Fair at Badr—Scandalous Marriage with Zainab—
Justified by "Revelation"—Ordinances for Women—The
Prophet's Exemptions—The Scandal raised against Ayesha,
who is cleared by a Revelation—Punishment of the Slanderers
—Laws for the Prophet's Wives—Medīna besieged by the
Quraish—The Ditch—Siege raised—Massacre of the Quraiza
Jewish Tribe—Minor Expeditions—Assassinations.

THE second battle of Badr, to which the Quraish had
defied Muhammad after Uhud, did not take place.
There was distress and scarcity in Mecca, and the
Meccans were unable to set a large force in the field.
They therefore bribed some desert Arabs to carry to
Medīna false tidings to terrify the people. But Muhammad was not deceived; he set out at the head of
1500 men, held for eight days a large fair at Badr, and
returned with honour and profit to Medīna; and he
published in the Qurān (iii. 173 *seq.*) a song of encouragement and triumph. No further attack was
made from Mecca till the siege a full year later, and
meanwhile Muhammad exercised his troops in various
minor expeditions, inuring them to war and hardship,
fostering their appetite for spoil, opening their eyes to
wider vistas of conquest in his cause, and spreading
through ever-widening areas the terror of his name.
On one of these minor expeditions he instituted the

"Service of Danger," by which part of the army was kept constantly under arms, lest they should be surprised while engaged in their religious duties: even so Ezra had provided at the rebuilding of Jerusalem more than a thousand years earlier.

While Muhammad enjoyed rest from his foes without, and his power within Medīna was growing more and more absolute and unquestioned, he further increased the number of his wives, and promulgated, as by divine authority, those ordinances on marriage, seclusion of women, and divorce, together with those exemptions personal to himself, which are among the darkest blots on his religion and his own character. Within a year he added to the three wives he already had three more —Zainab, widow of Ubaida, slain at Badr, called, from her great charity, "the mother of the poor"; Umm Salma, whose husband died of wounds received at Uhud; and Zainab, wife of Zaid, who divorced her that she might become Muhammad's wife. This Zaid was Muhammad's freedman and adopted son, one of his earliest and most attached followers, and his wife should have been as a daughter to the prophet: in Arab eyes (as in Hindu eyes to-day) she was his *daughter-in-law*, and to marry her was incest. Yet Muhammad, a man now of fifty-seven, saw her accidentally in undress when he went to her husband's house; the wife's vanity was flattered by his undisguised admiration; and the husband, learning what had happened, set her free to follow her fancy. It is right to say that the Prophet dissuaded Zaid, but his opposition cannot have been strong; he seized the opportunity to marry the divorced woman, and produced a divine commission for the act, wherein it was declared that adoption

created no real relationship, and that the conduct of
all concerned was highly pleasing to the Lord! Zaid
has in consequence the singular honour of being the
only man blessed by name in the Qurān, as Abu
Lahb has of being cursed therein; and Zainab claimed
a special glory as having been given by God to the
Prophet, whereas his other wives he had chosen for
himself. It was at this time, perhaps taught by his
own experience, that he issued (always as God's
spokesman) stringent regulations for the privacy of
his wives. No longer was the open hospitality of the
desert Arabs to be practised. Strangers were to come
very seldom to the Prophet's home: it must be remembered that he had no separate house of his own.
He passed his days in rotation at the houses of his
wives: visitors were to stay but a short time, and to
have their wants supplied from the household *separated
by a curtain*. All women were to be carefully veiled
before any but their nearest relatives, the Prophet's
privacy was specially guarded, and his absolute power
and discretion affirmed, and the darkest threats uttered
against any infidels who dared insult Muslim women.
Amongst the peculiar privileges enjoyed by the Prophet
was that of sharing his time as he pleased among his
wives, whilst other Muslims were bound to divide theirs
equally: and his wives were condemned after his death,
this also by revelation, to perpetual widowhood. We
shall see later some very striking uses of the intervention of the friendly Archangel Gabriel in the matter
of "revelations," even in matters of intimate private
concern. It is always to be remembered that Muhammad taught that the Qurān in its entirety existed
from the earliest age of eternity, being the first created

thing, or at least only second to the "Light of
Muhammad "; that it lay recorded at the throne of God
on the Preserved Tablet, until the time came for it to
be revealed; that it was then sent down to the lowest
heaven by the hand of Gabriel, and was by him thereafter given piecemeal to the Prophet by successive
instalments.   The consequences, and the advantages, of
this system are obvious !

   In this same year 626, in December, Muhammad led
a successful expedition against the Bani Mustaliq, who
were in league with his foes of Mecca.   He took with
him Ayesha and Umm Salma.   The attack was completely successful, and very large booty was taken.
But two very unfortunate events marred the campaign.
A quarrel broke out between the refugees and the
men of Medīna, which nearly led to serious bloodshed, and Abdullah ibn Ubai uttered ominous threats.
Muhammad averted the danger by breaking up his
camp, and so diverting the thoughts of the army.
The second matter which marred Muhammad's joy in
his return to Medīna was of a different and more serious
nature.   He had added to the number of his wives
Juwairiya, the beautiful widow of the slain chief of
the Bani Mustaliq, after himself paying to her captor
the large ransom required; but on the homeward
march, already disturbed by the quarrelsome spirit of
the men of Medīna and the threats of Abdallah,
occurred a second unfortunate incident, which for a
time threatened altogether to shipwreck his domestic
peace.

   It was Muhammad's custom to take with him on
his various expeditions from Medīna one or more of his
wives, chosen either by rotation or by lot.   On that

from which he had just returned his companions had been Umm Salma and Ayesha, the latter still very young as age is counted in the west, but blooming into womanhood in the sunnier regions of Arabia. She had now been seven years married to the Prophet, and was his favourite wife, as her father Abu Bakr was his dearest friend, as well as his wisest and most trusted counsellor. When death removed from his side the faithful Khadīja, not very long before Muhammad quitted Mecca, he supplied her place, as we have already seen, by marrying the widowed Sauda and Ayesha, who was still a child. The latter choice can only have been made from a desire to knit more closely the bonds by which he was already tied to his old friend, since, for some years to come, Ayesha, sprightly and winning though she was, could be no companion for him. In fact, the choice of a child for his wife was scandalous in the eyes even of his own followers, and still more in those of his countrymen generally. The marriage was not consummated for three years, and even then the child-wife had not yet cast away her dolls, and the Prophet helped her to play with them!

Now, however, she had for long been recognised as queen of his affections, a position that only Hafsa, daughter of Omar, sometimes challenged, but in vain. Ayesha was still very young, and too slight for her weight to be greatly felt in the covered litter which was swung on the camel which carried her. Now, on the day when Muhammad and his force marched into Medina, Ayesha's litter was found to be empty, and she herself was missing; but a few hours later one of Muhammad's adherents, Safwān, who had shared in the Flight, came into the city leading his camel, with

Ayesha seated thereon closely veiled, as the recent
ordinance required the Prophet's wives to be. The
explanation she gave of the matter was natural enough,
and there seems no reason for not accepting it, especially when her position and the circumstances are
considered. She had everything to lose and nothing to
gain by an intrigue, and there is no other occasion of
suspicion against her during all her long life. She said
that, having gone from her tent a short distance, she
had dropped a necklace which she valued. Missing it,
she again left her tent to search for it, and while she
was gone the litter was slung up on the camel, the
absence of her light weight not being noticed, and the
march was resumed. When she returned, not finding
her camel, she sat down on the ground, expecting them
to return for her. Meanwhile Safwān came up, having
also been detained. He was astonished to find Ayesha,
made his camel kneel, and turned away his head while
she mounted. He then made all haste after the army,
but could not overtake it, and so it happened that
Ayesha entered the city, and went into her house in
full view of a scandal-loving public.

Muhammad, whose conscience perhaps told him that
his recent marriage with Juwairiya, daughter of the
the slain Mustaliq chief, and a little earlier with
Zainab after her divorce by Zaid, had given special
cause of jealousy to Ayesha, was much disquieted by
the reports that came to his ears. His manner changed,
and his coldness so affected Ayesha that she fell ill,
and with her husband's consent went home to her
parents. The breach was welcomed by the enemies of
both parties, and the scandal was spread by Abdallah
ibn Ubai on the one hand, and by the poet Hassān, by

Mista, a relative of Abu Bakr, and Hamna, sister of Zainab. But at the end of a month Muhammad could bear the estrangement no longer, and rebuked the slanderers of both Ayesha and Safwān publicly from the Mosque pulpit. It was an unwarrantable invasion of his privacy to discuss the affairs of his family at all, and there was nothing against either of the slandered persons. However, he took counsel with Usāma (son of Baraka, the Prophet's nurse, and of Zaid), and with Ali, and examined Ayesha's maid. Usāma declared the whole story slanderous, the maid could say nothing against her mistress, but Ali—who perhaps thought only that "Cæsar's wife must be beyond suspicion"— seems to have taken a harsher view. At all events Ayesha believed he did so, and this was probably the cause of the hatred she ever afterwards bore him, such that she rode with Muāwiya's army when he and Ali fought for the Khalifate. Ali, she says, urged the Prophet to put her away, saying, "There is no lack of women from whom thou mayest replace her!"[1]

Thereupon Muhammad went straight to Abu Bakr's house and himself questioned Ayesha, whom he found plunged in grief. Her mother had sought in vain to comfort her, telling her that a favourite wife could not escape the envious calumnies of her rivals, and her father also was powerless to help her. But when Muhammad sat down beside her, and adjured her by God to confess and repent if what men laid to her charge was true, after a short silence, in the hope that

[1] After the battle of the Camel, however, Ali's chivalrous conduct touched her heart, and she said, "There befell between Ali and me only that which commonly befalls between a wife and her husband's kindred" (see p. 187).

her parents would answer for her, she passionately denied the charge. "I am helpless; I am guiltless, God knows. Yet none believeth my denial. *Patience becometh me, God is my helper!*" Muhammad's doubts vanished, but he perhaps knew that others would require stronger assurance. He affected to fall into a prophetic trance, and his hosts covered him up. After a little while he seemed to awake, wiped heavy drops of sweat from his brow, and cried, "Rejoice, Ayesha! Verily the Lord hath revealed thine innocence." And Ayesha answered, "Praise be to God!"

Then Muhammad went to the people, and declared to them the new revelation. They were sharply chidden for taking up and carrying the slander, which God Himself declared to be groundless. The law was laid down that fornication should be punished publicly with a hundred stripes; and to establish a charge of adultery against a married woman four witnesses were required, failing which the accusers were to be punished with fourscore stripes. A husband might establish a charge of adultery against his wife by a fourfold oath, with an imprecation of God's wrath upon himself if he lied; and it was open to the wife by similar oath to clear herself; but the husband's absolute right to divorce her was not affected. The Chapter warned the slanderers to repent, and to shun such calumny in future; and Abu Bakr was exhorted to continue his bounty to the offending Mista, his relative. The curse of God was solemnly pronounced on false accusers,— and then the earthly penalty of stripes was inflicted on all who had slandered Ayesha in this matter, excepting only Abdallah, against whom evidently Muhammad did not dare to proceed. With this punishment the Prophet was satisfied, and in particular he extended marked favour to the poet Hassān, who showed his gratitude in eloquent praises of Ayesha, with whom he was thenceforward closely bound.

The interest and importance of the story lies for us not in the question of Ayesha's guilt or innocence, though there seems small ground of suspicion against her, but in the light shed on Muhammad's character. He gave weight to the charge against her, and came to believe she was innocent. He punished her accusers severely, alleging the commands of God, and he imposed on his injured wife and on her father—his old friend Abu Bakr—with a simulated revelation. But he also took advantage of the incident to lay special further restrictions, in the name of God, on his own wives above those of other men (Sūra 33). He wrote:—

"O Prophet! say to thy wives, 'If ye desire the life of this world and its adornments, come, I will give you them to enjoy, and will send you away richly endowed! But if ye desire God and His apostle and the life to come, verily God hath prepared for those of you who do well a mighty reward.

"O wives of the Prophet! whosoever of you commits open sin, doubled shall be her torment twice,—and that is easy unto God!

"But she among you who cleaveth fast to God and His apostle and doeth righteousness, to her will we give her reward twice told, and for her have we prepared a noble provision.

"O ye wives of the Prophet! ye are not like unto other women. If ye fear God be not too complaisant in speech, lest he in whose heart is a disease desire you; but speak well-ordered speech.

8

"Abide ye within your houses, and set not off your-selves as in past days of Ignorance; but be ye stead-fast in prayer, and give alms, and obey God and His apostle. Verily the Lord desires only to put away abomination from you, ye that are of His house, and thoroughly to purify you!

"And remember what is recited in your houses of the signs of God and wisdom; verily God is subtle and all-knowing."

Then Ayesha resumed her ascendency over the Prophet's heart, only the more powerful for the tem-porary breach; and the Prophet fenced his household round with an impenetrable veil of ceremony and decorum. The name of God was used, and His power usurped, to guard the virtue of Muhammad's wives, and the divine sanction was annexed to the new ordinances for the enslavement of women to man's caprice!

Muhammad was now called to meet a formidable attack from without. The Quraish, enraged at the insult flung in their teeth by the fair held at Badr, had gathered a great host from Mecca and the allied desert tribes, and advanced on Medīna in such strength as to compel the citizens to withdraw within their walls. This time Muhammad's wise plans were heartily sup-ported by all; by the advice of a Persian prisoner, Salmān, a great trench was dug to complete the de-fences of the city; the Prophet himself laboured among the rest; pick, and shovel, and basket were plied with unflagging zeal, while he blessed, en-couraged, and shared the toil; and in six days the ditch was ready, whilst a battery of stones was laid to hand against assault. It was in fact the *agger*

and *vallum* with which every Roman camp was protected.

The enemy, 10,000 strong, ravaged the country
round, and advanced against the city, only to be baffled
by the new defence. They then endeavoured to gain
over to their side the only remaining Jewish tribe, the
Quraiza, who occupied a walled village in the outskirts
of the city. Whether the Jews did agree to join them
or not is doubtful. The evidence is entirely that of
their enemies, they had strong grounds for hostility to
Muhammad, and he and his followers had (in the light
of after events) every reason to blacken them : in any
case they took no overt part in the attack. Muhammad's
small army of 3000 men camped within the ditch, two
strong bodies patrolled the streets night and day, and
the vigilance of the defenders repulsed every minor
attack. Two determined general assaults were made
on successive days ; but the garrison, though sorely
bestead, beat them both off. The valour of Ali
especially, and the galling hail of the archers, aided
by the wide and deep ditch, kept back even the fiery
and skilful attacks of Khālid. But the city was in
terrible straits, and the courage of the Muslims almost
failed. Muhammad tried first to detach the Bedouin
allies from his enemies, but could not bribe high
enough,—and the siege went on for a fortnight. At
the end of that time he succeeded in sowing distrust
among the confederates, who were already straitened
from want of supplies ; again the elements came to
Muhammad's aid, and a great storm burst over the
besieging army ; Abu Sufiyān broke up his camp, and
the siege was at an end.

Muhammad had no thought of pursuit, but he

resolved by an act of terrible punishment to destroy
the last remnants of opposition at home. He had not
yet cleansed himself from the dust of battle, when he
ordered Bilāl to gather the host to the great Mosque;
the banner of Islām was placed in Ali's hands, and the
whole army—3000 strong—was led forth against the
fortress of the Quraiza, which was invested. Ill-provided
against a siege, the unhappy Jews soon asked for terms,
but no terms would be granted. A friend warned them
to expect no mercy, and at last, after a despairing defence
of fifteen days, they surrendered at discretion, it being
agreed that their sentence should be pronounced by
Saad, of the Bani Aus, with whom they had been
formerly in alliance. Again was shown the awful
truth that "Islām had broken all old ties." His tribesmen interceded in vain with Saad for the 2000
hapless Jews, men, women, and children; brought with
difficulty from the bed on which he lay from a wound
gotten in the siege, he surveyed the trembling crowd
with unpitying eye, and passed the doom: "The men
to the slaughter, the remnant to slave-market, and the
spoil to the army." The Prophet approved: Saad, he
said, had pronounced the judgment of God in the
seventh heaven; trenches were dug as common graves;
and on the morrow the men of the tribe, to the number
of 700, were butchered in cold blood under Muhammad's
own eyes. He himself took the "royal fifth" of the
captives and the spoil, the women and children were
sold into slavery, and the booty divided; and a beautiful Jewess, Rihāna, was forced to be the Prophet's
concubine, as she refused to forsake her religion and
become his wife.

No words can fittingly condemn the bloody cruelty

of this massacre; every reader will judge of it for himself; yet not a word of pity for the victims, or blame for the actors, comes from a Muslim historian. For us the last touches of horror are added by the fact that Muhammad declared he had been called to the assault by Gabriel himself, and that when Saad soon after died of his wound, he prayed over him and blessed his memory, and declared that the heavenly host helped to carry the bier. Thus was the Prophet's power at last established absolutely in Medīna: the time had now come when he would prepare the way for that conquest of Mecca, of which he had long dreamed.

The following year was spent in minor forays or expeditions, led either by Muhammad himself or by some trusted lieutenant: some were punitive, but others unprovoked attacks for purposes of plunder. In one of the former, led by Zaid, an aged woman, Umm Kirfa, was put to death in a cruel and barbarous manner, but no censure was passed on the horrid deed. A rich Meccan caravan was cut off and plundered at Al Is, as it passed north to Syria along the Red Sea shore; and among the captives was Muhammad's own son-in-law, Abul Aas, nephew of Khadīja and husband of Zainab. Husband and wife were deeply attached, but Abul Aas had not embraced Islām, and Zainab had stayed behind with him in Mecca. He had already been taken prisoner at Badr, and set free by Muhammad for love of Khadīja's memory, but on condition that Zainab should be sent to Medīna. This was done, but she suffered grave mischief as she set out, for which afterwards bloody vengeance was taken. On this occasion, too, the captors let Abul Aas free and restored his property for Muhammad's sake; he joined the new faith, and settled in Medīna. Another expedition is notable as the first communication with the Roman Empire. An envoy to Syria, who had been favourably received, was returning to Muhammad, when he was attacked and robbed; and Zaid inflicted severe punishment on the marauders. This was followed by an expedition against Dūmat al Jandal (now Jauf),[1] where the Christian tribes were offered the choice of Islām or tribute; some chose one and some the other alternative, —and this marks a further step in Muhammad's progress to empire. There remain to be noticed in this period the treacherous murder of Abdul Haqīq, a Jewish chief, at Khaibar, for having taken part in the siege of Medīna, and on suspicion of further hostile designs. His successor in the chiefship, together with thirty followers, was also foully murdered, while their murderers were actually taking them under safe-conduct to treat with Muhammad at Medīna. All these treacherous assassinations were solemnly approved by the Prophet; nay, he himself actually sent a well-known bravo to murder his old enemy Abu Sufiyān in Mecca, though it is alleged (without much proof) that this was in retaliation for a similar attack from Abu Sufiyān: the attempt on Muhammad's life is said to have been defeated through a revelation from on high, but his own emissary was recognised as a notorious murderer, and in his escape murdered two (or three) defenceless tribesmen; the former became a good Muslim, and the latter was welcomed home by the Prophet.

[1] The first stage of Palgrave's adventurous journey in 1863.

CHAPTER IX

Now, after six full years of exile, Muhammad and his followers from Mecca longed with a great longing after their native city, and to take their part once more in pilgrimage and its hallowed rites; and in a dream he saw that the desire of their hearts had been granted them. The month was one of peace — Zu'l Qada — in which the Lesser Pilgrimage could fitly be performed, so (in February 628), after inviting, but without much success, the neighbouring tribes to join with him, Muhammad set forth at the head of 1500 men. Elated with the promise of success, the great army marched trustfully forward; seventy camels were devoted for the sacrifice. As they approached the sacred territory, all assumed the *ihrām*, the pilgrim's garb, and shouted, "Labbaik! Labbaik! Here are we, O Lord!" They marched with no weapons save sheathed swords, and had no thought of fighting. But the Meccans were resolved

119

to oppose them. A large army was gathered, and the Medīna road blocked, the leaders being Khālid and Ikrima, and the troops wearing leopard skins, to show they would conquer or die.

On hearing this news Muhammad turned aside to Hudaibiya, on the border of Meccan territory, and there encamped. At first he was minded to fight in order to accomplish his purpose, but after messengers had passed to and fro, and he found the Quraish absolutely resolved not to permit the pilgrimage, he yielded. In the negotiations which followed, he showed great skill; the envoys of the Quraish were one and all impressed by the state he held and the devotion of his followers, and the impression then made was of no small use afterwards. The Quraish absolutely refused to allow the pilgrimage to be carried out that year, but were willing it should be performed the next. So a regular treaty was drawn up, and Muhammad was thereby recognised as a power in Arabia of equal standing with the state of Mecca. Some dispute arose as to the preamble, but the Prophet yielded on all unessential points, and the treaty was duly ratified, the original remaining with him, and a copy being given to the Quraish. It was agreed that—(1) war should cease for ten years; (2) tribes and individuals should be free to ally themselves with either party; (3) minors going from the Quraish to Muhammad, without consent of their guardians, should be sent back; but (4) followers of Muhammad returning to the Quraish should not be sent back; (5) Muhammad and his followers should not enter Mecca this year, but might do so unarmed for three days next year, and perform the pilgrimage. The abortive pilgrimage on which they had started was so far fulfilled that the victims were slain and the pilgrims shaved their heads, and the Prophet and his followers went back to Medīna.

The success gained was great, and on the way back Muhammad was "inspired" to celebrate his "evident victory" from the Lord (Sura 48). His followers, who had expected to fulfil the pilgrimage unhindered, and who were inclined to murmur, were satisfied and encouraged; severe rebuke was dealt to the tribes who had refused to march with them, and they were debarred from sharing future adventures; while special blessings were pronounced on "the men of the Tree," who had pledged themselves to vengeance, when it was feared that Muhammad's envoy — Uthmān — had been treacher-ously murdered in Mecca. The fruits of the treaty also soon showed themselves in the adhesion of scattered converts from Mecca, some of whom were surrendered under it, and some not; and the whole of the Khuzāa tribe embraced Islām. Moreover, Muhammad now felt so sure of himself and his power, that he resolved to summon all neighbouring potentates to accept his mission,—Rome, Persia, Abyssinia, Syria, Egypt, and Yamāma; and to authenticate the credentials of his envoys, he caused a silver seal to be made, graven with the words, "Muhammad the Apostle of God."[1]

The despatch to the Roman Emperor (Heraclius) reached him in the floodtide of success against Persia, and no reply was vouchsafed; nor was the vassal chief of Ghassān allowed to reply. The Persian king tore the summons scornfully in pieces, but he himself was soon after slain, and his governor of Yaman ac-knowledged the Prophet's claims. In Egypt the envoy

[1] See Appendix.

was received with honour, though the governor cour-
teously declined to acknowledge Muhammad's claims;
but he sent him the present of two beautiful sisters as
slaves, and a valuable white mule. The mule was taken
for the Prophet's own riding, and the fairer of the two
sisters, Mary the Copt, was placed in his harem, the
other—Shīrīn—being bestowed on the poet Hassān,
quite lately slanderer of Ayesha, but now her staunch
friend. A similar courteous reply came from the Prince
of Abyssinia, who also gave Umm Habība, widow of one
of the Meccan exiles, to Muhammad to wife, and sent
back with honour all the exiles who had not already
joined him in Medīna. The last messenger was met
with a singular claim to share the power, a claim which
was promptly rejected; and the daring pretender was
heartily cursed, and died in the following year!

The return of the exiles remaining in Abyssinia, however, had been preceded by the final accomplishment of
Muhammad's vengeance against the Jews. To reward
his followers after the unfulfilled pilgrimage, he had
promised them success and rich spoil; and accordingly,
in August 628, he set out from Medīna at the head of
1600 men; he made three forced marches of great
length, and fell unexpectedly on the rich Jewish settlement of Khaibar. Taken by surprise, the little forts
that studded the fertile valley fell one by one; a rally
was made before Qāmus, and the attack was led by dauntless Ali; prodigies of valour were performed, the desperate courage of the Jews served them nothing, Qāmus
was surrendered, and Kināna, the chief, gave himself up
along with his cousin. Muhammad, having found
occasion against them for concealing some of their
treasure, had them cruelly tortured and then beheaded;

and again he celebrated his triumph by taking as his wife Sāfia the beautiful widow of hapless and gallant Kināna. Sāfia submitted to her new lot, it is said, gladly; but Zainab, another woman of the tribe, who had lost husband and father and uncle in the fighting, took terrible vengeance. She dressed a kid for the feast, steeped it in deadly poison, and set it before the Prophet and his friends. One died, and Muhammad himself was violently ill, and attributed his last sickness (three years later) to the effects of the poison.[1] The murderess was put to death. The remaining strongholds of Khaibar surrendered, and the immense booty enriched every man of the army. Half the lands of Khaibar also were portioned out among them, the other half being assigned as a sort of crown domain to Muhammad; stringent laws were laid down against embezzlement of booty; and some ceremonial ordinances regarding unclean meats were promulgated. Then with an army enriched, and a new wife for himself, the Prophet returned to Medīna, welcomed back the exiles from Abyssinia, and celebrated fresh nuptials with Umm Habība, his *ninth* wife!

After a quiet half year in Medīna, broken only by some minor expeditions, the time came round when by treaty the pilgrimage might be performed, and three days might be spent in Mecca. In February 629, Muhammad started, with a following now grown to 2000 men, unarmed save with sheathed swords, and with sixty camels for the sacrifice; the Quraish, to avoid all chance of conflict, withdrew to the neighbouring hills,

---

[1] One of the extravagant late-invented tales to exalt the Prophet is, that the poisoned kid's flesh cried out from the dish, warning him not to touch it!

and looked curiously on, while the mighty cavalcade swept into the vacant city. It was a solemn occasion, and the hearts of the exiles thrilled with emotion, as they followed their beloved leader to perform the hallowed rites from which they had so long been debarred. "Labbaik! Labbaik!" they cried; the Prophet touched with his staff the thrice-holy Black Stone, which many years before he had guided to its place in the temple wall; seven times he rode round the Holy House, and seven times his followers compassed it—three times at racing speed, and four at more sober pace;[1] and he stilled the shout of defiance they began, and bade them instead cry aloud: "There is no God but the Lord alone! It is He that hath holden His servant and exalted his army! Alone hath He discomfited the confederate hosts!" Then they made the passage seven times between Safā and Marwā, slaughtered the victims, and shaved their heads; and at length the pilgrimage was accomplished.

The next day Muhammad passed the forenoon in prayer at the Kaaba, and at noon loud-voiced Bilāl summoned the host to public prayer in the sacred precincts, and the Prophet led their devotions. During the three days of his stay, he entered no house in Mecca, but abode in a tent; there he received such of the citizens as came to him, and his courteous and winning ways had their effect. At the suggestion of his uncle Abbās, whose widowed sister-in-law she was, he arranged to marry Maimūna, and the marriage was celebrated at

[1] This is still the custom, as Burton found. Tradition says Muhammad directed it to be so, that the Quraish might see how little the climate of Medīna had relaxed the Muslims' strength! Each time the pilgrim passes the Black Stone he kisses it, if possible, but, if not, he touches it with his hand, which he then kisses.

the first stage on the retreat from Mecca, as the Quraish roughly insisted that the three days stay should not be exceeded. Maimūna was at this time fifty-one, and this marriage was Muhammad's last. It had important political consequences, for Maimūna was aunt to the mighty warrior Khālid, who shortly after embraced Islām, and was followed by Amru, a poet and man of counsel, famous in after days as the conqueror of Egypt, and by Uthmān, custodian of the Kaaba. Thus was the Prophet's cause advanced in Mecca, while the power of the Quraish correspondingly declined.

In the year that followed, the fortunes of Muhammad were chequered. He inflicted punishment on various tribes, in one case sending forth his commander with instructions "not to let a soul escape," which order was obeyed to the letter. But the great event of the year was the disastrous battle of Mūta, when the small Arab army of 3000 men met the legions of Heraclius. They had been sent, under Zaid's command, to avenge the murder of an envoy, and were dismissed by Muhammad from the "Mount of Farewell" with the blessing: "The Lord shield you from every evil, and bring you back in peace laden with spoil!" Zaid, who had thought to meet only a desert tribe of the Syrian border, came upon the whole Imperial army strongly posted at the southern extremity of the Dead Sea.

A halt was called and a council of war held, but the bolder counsel prevailed; the army again went forward, and awaited attack. The Roman army, Arab horse on either flank, swept on and enveloped the little host; Zaid, with the Prophet's white banner in one hand, fought bravely in the foremost ranks and fell. Jafar and Abdallah, appointed to command in succession after him, emulated his bravery and likewise fell; after which Khālid, raised by general voice to the command, collected the scattered remnant of the routed army, and by skilful leading brought them back to Medīna. Some of the people murmured at the retreat, but Muhammud welcomed the brave, though beaten, troops and their leaders, and cheered them with words of hope; but deeply he mourned for his devoted friend Zaid and the others who had fallen, and comforted and relieved their sorrowing families.

The disaster of Mūta was soon avenged by Amru, who marched rapidly with 300, reinforced later to 500, men to the Syrian border. The Roman forces retired before him, the frontier tribes gave in their submission, and the power of Muhammad was greatly extended and confirmed. The terror of his arms was much helped by his courteous reception of all who came in, and his fame for power and clemency spread through Arabia.

The following year, 630, crowned Muhammad with the conquest of Mecca. A ground of quarrel was furnished by an attack by allies of the Quraish on the Khuzāa, who had joined Muhammad. To him they at once appealed, and he seized the opportunity: "If I help you not as strongly as though the cause were mine own, never more may the Lord help me in my need!" he exclaimed. The news was carried to Mecca, and the Meccans in terror sent Abu Sufiyān to heal the breach; but he returned without success.

Muhammad gathered his hosts for attack, but masked his object. A woman was sent secretly to warn the Quraish, but was captured and brought

back, and on the 1st January 630, 10 Ramadhān,
A.H. 8, the great host set forward for the conquest of
the Holy City. The desert allies were called up and
swelled the army with warriors, till at the head of
well-nigh 10,000 men Muhammad pushed on by forced
marches, encamping, ere more than a week was past,
at the last stage before Mecca; while, as a first-fruit
of his success, his uncle Abbās came out and enrolled
himself amongst his followers. So swift and secret
had been the advance that the Quraish were in ignorance of their danger, and Abu Sufiyān, sent forth to
reconnoitre, was astounded by the blaze of countless
camp-fires on the heights surrounding Mecca. Abbās
met him, and led him to the Prophet's tent, but he was
not admitted to an audience until the morrow. It was
then too late to make terms; a short, stormy interview
ended by his embracing Islām; and then he was sent
back to the city, with the promise that none who sought
refuge with him, or at the Kaaba, or that stayed in
their own houses, should be harmed. The chief went
back, and as he passed through the warlike host, he
clearly saw that the Prophet's day of triumph had
dawned.

As the conqueror's terms were proclaimed, the
affrighted citizens fled in all directions to seek
asylum; the army marched on the unresisting city;
the various divisions advanced by their appointed
roads; every possible precaution was taken to avoid
bloodshed,—and only one skirmish took place, between
Khālid's force and a desperate band of Meccans. Otherwise the advance was unopposed; and Muhammad,
preceded by the Refugees, passed into the valley, not
far from the tombs of Khadīja and Abu Tālib, and

pitched his tent just outside the city on the north, the great white standard being reared beside it. Soon he again came forth, mounted Al Qaswā, and rode to the Kaaba. There he first touched the Black Stone with his staff, and then commanded that the temple should be cleansed from its idols. They fell one by one at his word, and last of all the great image of Hubal, chief tutelary deity of Mecca; as that crashed to the ground, he said, "Truth is come, and falsehood is vanished away; for verily lying is but for a moment!" Then he worshipped at the Station of Abraham, and commanded the door of the Temple to be opened to him; next, standing on the threshold, he exercised the first acts of authority by returning the keys to Uthmān as hereditary guardian, and confirming to his uncle Abbās the right of supplying the pilgrims with water. The inside of the Temple also was cleansed from all idolatrous taint, and then the Prophet gave vent to the deep love he bore to his native city: "Thou art the choicest portion of the earth to me, and the most lovable: had I not been cast forth, never should I have forsaken thee." The citizens were won by his words, and then he turned to them of Medīna and said, "God forbid that I should leave *you*; where ye live will I live too, and there will I die!"

Muhammad now showed himself as generous in victory as he had been resolute to have submission. He proclaimed a general amnesty, from which only ten or twelve persons were excluded, and of them only four were actually put to death. Even Abdallah, the renegade secretary, with Hind, the ferocious wife of Abu Sufiyān, Ikrima, and Safwān were forgiven on professing Islām.

Thus was Mecca conquered almost without bloodshed; the citizens turned heartily to their new master and his religion; and the great shrine and idols of the surrounding tribes were destroyed almost without opposition. Only Khālid shed innocent blood, and Muhammad made amends for it, though he could not dismiss his able but savage lieutenant.

Muhammad's repose was soon rudely broken. The great and warlike tribe of Hawāzin, whose wide territories lay towards the north-east of Mecca, moved by fear or jealousy of his power, mustered their forces to attack him; and just four weeks after he had left Medīna, he marched against them at the head of 12,000 men, of whom 2000 were Meccans. The two armies met at the valley of Hunain, but Mālik, the Hawāzin leader, had seized the narrow entrance to it and laid an ambush; so confident was he of victory that, against the advice of his old counsellor Duraid, he brought with him the women and children, the flocks and the herds of the clan. Khālid led the Muslim advance, but his troops fell into the ambush; they were thrown back, and the whole army began to flee in wild confusion. By the utmost personal exertion, the most passionate appeals, Muhammad rallied his forces; they turned again fiercely to the attack, and desperately stormed the heights; at the critical moment the Prophet, as before at Badr, cast a handful of gravel against the foe, crying, "Ruin seize them!" and again, "I swear by the Lord of the Kaaba! God hath cast fear into their hearts." The enemy wavered, broke, and fled in headlong rout; and though Mālik with the rearguard covered the flight, his camp, with women, children,

9

cattle, and stores, fell into the hands of the Muslims. The pursuit was pressed, and the rout completed, but not without severe loss to the victors. But though the army was dispersed, a large part of it had fallen back into Tā,if, a fortified town, to which Muhammad at once laid regular siege. It was vigorously carried on, and engines of war brought up, but in vain; even the fruit-trees, for which the town has always been famous, were destroyed; but the garrison held out, and the siege was raised.

The booty, stored during the siege, was now divided, and this was done with such wise liberality as to win over many of Muhammad's powerful foes; the men of Medīna, murmuring over the favour shown to Meccans, were again won over by appeal to their devotion; even Mālik, the Hawāzin chief, was converted to Islām by the wise generosity shown him. Most touching of all, however, is the story of how the captives were set free. The Bani Saad, among whom Muhammad had been fostered, were a branch of the Hawāzin, and one of the prisoners was his own foster-sister. She made good her claim, was kindly treated, and sent back with rich gifts to her people; the ties of fosterage were then pressed by the people generally, and liberally allowed; and in the end all the prisoners were set free by their captors, Muhammad himself paying their ransom where any was demanded. He then again performed the Lesser Pilgrimage and returned to Medīna, leaving, as his deputy in Mecca, Attāb, a young and wise Quraishite, and Mu,āz to instruct the citizens in the Qurān and the duties of religion.

On his return to Medīna, the Prophet was bereaved of his daughter Zainab; Ruqāya he had lost when

Badr was fought, and now Fātima only was left. But great joy followed, for Mary, the Coptic girl sent him from Egypt, bore him a son, whom he named Ibrāhīm. Naturally the tenderness of his love for the child was unbounded, and overflowed to the mother. He showed her special favour, to the neglect even of Ayesha and Hafsa, and these two naturally resented it. Was it to be endured that the daughters of his two most powerful supporters, both in the prime of womanhood, both sprung from the bluest blood of the Quraish, should be set aside for an Abyssinian slave-girl?

Muhammad had owed to Mary the Copt the greatest happiness of his later years, in the birth of Ibrāhīm, the child of his old age, and the early loss of the little one was the deepest grief he could suffer. Not one of his many wives, since he lost Khadīja, had borne him a child, and of his children by her only one daughter now survived—Fātima, wife of Ali, in whose two sons, Hasan and Husain, now lay the sole hope of the continuance of his race. It is easy, therefore, to understand how his heart had been bound up in the boy, and how greatly he loved the mother. And so it befell that he was involved in the last and perhaps the worst scandal of his life, through the jealousy which is inseparable from the practice of polygamy. The story is most unpleasant to tell, but it is generally accepted and told without a word of censure by the chief commentators on the Qurān, and by most of the Prophet's biographers, and their attitude towards it is typical of their general position in regard to him. Possessing, as they hold, every virtue in the highest degree, his every action is praiseworthy; everything done in his service or for his sake is to be commended, and no breath of censure is to blow upon his life.

When Mary had come, together with her sister Shīrīn, to Muhammad, he had not *married* her, and it seems doubtful whether she had embraced Islām, though one tradition says that he chose her for himself rather than her sister because she was the first to pronounce the confession of faith. He gave her also a separate dwelling, a little house in a garden, and there he used to visit her. As we have seen, he had, when he came to Medīna, built no separate house for himself, but his wives had each her own, the whole forming a row of little dwellings facing the Mosque; and he used to spend a day with each in rotation, taking with him the few things necessary for his personal comfort. He had been by "revelation" freed from the obligation to divide his time strictly among his wives, but he had not availed himself of the privilege. One day, however, when it was Hafsa's turn, she went to spend the day with her parents, and he passed the time in Hafsa's own apartment with Mary. Hafsa returned unexpectedly, and found the door locked, so that she could not gain admittance till Muhammad came out. She then went in, found Mary, and threatened to make the scandal and insult to herself public. To appease her righteous indignation Muhammad swore that he would not again see Mary, but he solemnly bound Hafsa to keep the matter secret. Hafsa, however, who was very intimate with Ayesha, could not refrain from revealing the matter to her, and she appears to have betrayed her knowledge to Muhammad.

He was very angry that the matter should have got abroad, declared himself at once free from his oath, and proceeded to punish all his wives, by forsaking their society altogether and spending a whole month in the company of Mary. At the end of that time, however, the situation became intolerable; Abu Bakr and Omar were beyond measure grieved at the scandal in which their daughters were involved, and Muhammad determined to end it. As on the former occasion with Ayesha, so now he pretended that Gabriel intervened with a message from on high, bidding him forgive Hafsa on her repentance; the forgiveness was naturally extended to all the rest, and matters resumed their former course in his relations with his wives.

The offence of Hafsa lay in her betrayal of Muhammad's secret, to which Ayesha had become a party by receiving the confidence, and the two together were guilty of disobedience to the Prophet, little better than high treason. Nothing is told us of offence given by the other wives (of whom there were seven), and we are driven to think that Muhammad was glad of a pretext to indulge for a time exclusively his passion for Mary. He again promulgated a chapter of the Qurān, confirming and extending his own power and privileges, and setting forth his singular position as the favourite and confidant of Heaven. Palmer, in his note on the Chapter (64), accepts without question the story of Hafsa's wrong and her betrayal of the secret, and explains that it "is intended to free him from his oath respecting Mary, and to reprove his wives for their conduct"; it runs:—

"O Prophet, wherefore dost thou forbid to thyself what God has made lawful to thee, seeking to please thy wives? but God is forgiving, compassionate!

"God has allowed you to expiate your oaths; for God is your King, and He is all-knowing wise!

"And when the Prophet told as a secret to one of his wives a recent thing, and when she told thereof and exposed it, he acquainted her of part, and part he kept back.

"But when he informed her of it, she said, 'Who told thee this?' he said, 'The Wise, the Well-aware informed me.

"'If ye both turn penitent unto God,—for your hearts have swerved! (Well!)—but if ye support one another against him,—verily, God, He is King; and Gabriel and the righteous of the believers, and the angels after that, will support him.

"'It may be that his Lord, if he divorce you, will give him, in exchange, wives better than you,—Muslims, believers, devout, repentant, prayerful, given to fasting, —such as have been wedded, and virgins too.'"

The reference to the "part concealed" by the Prophet in his upbraiding of his peccant wife is obscure, and one tradition makes it refer to his telling Ayesha and Hafsa that first Abu Bakr and then Omar should succeed to his power after his death: the story is unlikely, and the tradition weak. Probably enough, it was invented to counterbalance those which alleged that Ali had been designated as successor. Another tradition interprets the "promise," from which the Prophet was absolved, as one to refrain from eating honey, flavoured with a certain strong-smelling shrub; but this explanation is very generally rejected, and seems on the face of it absurd. The "faithful" were by this time quite used to the interposition of Gabriel and divine revelation in the Prophet's domestic affairs, and their robust belief was not staggered by this last instance of it.

Yet it is difficult to find words for the awful blasphemy, the daring impiety which would drag into a story of incontinence and vulgar jealousy the name and the commands of the Almighty, the God—as Muhammad taught—of unapproachable and ineffable holiness! It casts on the self-styled Prophet the deepest and darkest stain. It may here be noted that the remainder of the chapter, of which the verses relevant to the affair of Mary have been quoted, consists of eloquent and awful warnings to repentance, strengthened by promises of reward and threats of punishment, and by illustrations of the blessed and the accursed women of ancient sacred history or legend,—the wives of Noah and of Lot, the queen of Pharaoh and the Virgin Mary!

By the birth of her son Ibráhím, so named doubtless after the "Father of the Faithful," whose religion Muhammad professed to restore, Mary was raised above the ordinary status of a slave. She was no longer subject to sale by her master (a merciful provision which even our own generation remembers did not exist in the Slave States of America), and at his death would be entitled to her freedom.

But the Prophet was not to be blessed for any length of time with male offspring. For the first year of his life Ibráhím throve well, his father visited him daily at the house of his foster-mother, and loved to have him on his knees; but the little life soon dwindled away, and to his unspeakable grief this last son too was lost to Muhammad. His sorrow seemed even excessive to his followers, some of whom ventured to upbraid him; but he heeded them not. He laid the little body tenderly in the grave with his own hands, and blessed the child, saying, "The days of thy nursing shall be accomplished in paradise." Then he went home, and comforted the bereaved mother; and the faithful nurse he dowered with a fair garden of palm-trees.

CHAPTER X

MUHAMMAD, Prophet-Prince of Medīna and conqueror
of Mecca, was now, by his victory at Hunain, the chief
power in Arabia. By his skill in weaving into the
new faith the immemorial superstitions of Arabia, the
worship at the Kaaba, and the annual pilgrimage to
Mecca, he had established his spiritual power on a firm
basis; and in Islām secular authority was inextricably
bound up with it. Obedience to God and to His Prophet was the keystone of the arch, and that obedience
must be absolute and unconditional. We have seen
more than once to what lengths the devotion of his
followers went. All old ties, however sacred, were
severed if they conflicted with the Prophet's commands;
secret murder, treacherous attack, abuse of hospitality,
—all were praiseworthy if practised in his service.
He had already made laws on most of the great interests
of civil and domestic life, he had secured, by his
generosity, his clemency, and his power, the hearts of
his people, and the finances of his state were firmly
grounded in the principles of the "royal fifth" and the

tithe of the increase, given to sanctify the believer's wealth.

His first step now was to send out regular collectors to gather in the tribute. This was, in almost every case promptly and cheerfully paid, but the tribe of Tamūsa made opposition. They were at once sharply punished, and many prisoners brought in to Medīna. The tribe sent envoys to make submission, and to redeem the captives, and succeeded, after professing Islām. After a contest, thoroughly Arab in spirit, in eloquence, they confessed themselves vanquished, and submitted without reserve. Muhammad took occasion, from the loud freedom of their address, to forbid such liberties for the future, and to direct that the Prophet should be addressed only in low, respectful tones, as became his high office and dignity. His receptions were held in the great Mosque, and there, in the presence of the people, he received deputations, gave judgments, and issued his sovereign commands. The want of outward state in no way lessened the reality of his power, and his sway was absolute and daily extending: from Yaman and Hadramaut and Omān, from the borders of Syria and Persia, envoys crowded to own his power and secure his favour. Among individual converts of note must be named Adi, son of Hātim, the famous chief of Tai, together with his tribe, half idolatrous and half Christian, and Kāb, son of Zuhair, the famous poet of Mecca. This ninth year after the Flight is known in Muslim annals specially as the "year of deputations."

At this time rumours of great preparations by the Roman power against him reached Muhammad at Medīna, and he resolved to strike the first blow. The

way was long and desert, and many refused the call to
arms. Some, especially men of Medína, were exempted,
but the desert tribes were straitly commanded to
join the army. Great enthusiasm was shown by the
majority, and the money contributions were most
liberal; many volunteers too had to be refused, as
they could not be mounted and equipped; and soon
Muhammad took the field at the head of the largest
army he had ever led,—no less (it is said) than 30,000
men, of whom 10,000 were horse. They marched
north through the arid valley of Hajar, but were
forbidden to drink of its wells, lest they should be
partakers in the sins of the old inhabitants, the impious
tribe of Thamúd. Thence they passed on to Tabúk,
not far from the Gulf of Ayla, and found the rumours
of invasion false. Accordingly Muhammad detached
Khálid with a strong body of cavalry against the
Christian chief of Dúma (Jauf), who was surprised
and brought in to Medína, where he embraced Islám;
the other Christian chiefs, and especially John, Prince
of Ayla, submitted to the Prophet himself at Tabúk,
and received from him letters of protection and treaties
of alliance, fixing their tribute, and taking them bound
to help all Muslim travellers and traders.

Muhammad then returned from Tabúk to Medína,
and declared the famous ninth Sura, the last in time of
the Qurán. Therein he rebuked and denounced those
who had shrunk from sharing the toil, the "Hypocrites" of Medína, and the desert Arabs; but those who
repented were forgiven, and after due chastisement
received back into favour. Then, too, he razed to the
ground a mosque that had been built, with sectarian
views, at Qubá; and pronounced God's curse against

the builders. At this time death removed Abdallah ibn Ubai, the Khazraj chief, who would, but for Muhammad s coming, have been king in Medīna. Him the Prophet had always treated with respect, though he never felt sure of his allegiance, and now he prayed over him, and walked behind the bier. Abdallah's influence, so far as we know, had always been exercised for good, and more than once had checked Muhammad in his revenge against the Jews.

The submission of Tā,if has now to be told. After the siege was raised, the chief Urwa came in to Medīna and joined Islām, and then, though dissuaded by Muhammad, he went to preach it to his own people. They slew him, but were soon reduced by Mālik to such straits that they sent an embassy of submission. The envoys were well-received; Muhammad himself taught them his doctrine; and at length they were sent back firm in the faith. It was not without vain struggles for delay, however, that they yielded to the destruction of their great idol Lāt, and to the " degradation" of the daily prayers,—which the Prophet declared to be indispensable.

He now resolved finally to clear Mecca from all taint of idolatry, and for that purpose he sent Abu Bakr to lead the annual Pilgrimage, and Ali to declare the Prophet's will at its close. So when the multitudes were gathered on the plain of Minā, Ali read the ordinance, forming part of the ninth Sura. The Prophet proclaimed himself free from all treaty obligations to idolaters; after four months, Believers were free to make war upon them wheresoever they should find them; no more should they take part in pilgrimage to the Holy House, nor profane it with pagan usages. The same chapter contains Muhammad's declaration of war against Jews and Christians; he needed them no more, for his own system, so largely borrowed from theirs, was now established; and to them was now left only the choice of submission or the sword.

During the two years that followed, embassies of submission came in from every side, and where there was still opposition to Islām it was crushed. Najrān yielded to the arms of Khālid, and the recalcitrant tribes of Yaman to those of Ali. The latter just completed his work in time to join Muhammad on his Farewell Pilgrimage to Mecca, in March 632, three months only before his death.

The city and temple of Mecca had been in the previous year completely purged of idolatry, and by Ali's proclamation idolaters were debarred from sharing in the Pilgrimage. The time was ripe for Muhammad to lead it solemnly himself, to lay down the complete ritual to be observed in ages to come, and to take—as it proved, and as perhaps he expected—solemn leave of the assembled people, as Moses had done, and Joshua and Samuel. So when the sacred season again returned, the month Zu'l Hijj, "first of months," when the Greater Pilgrimage [1] with its fuller rites should be performed, Muhammad set out, accompanied on this occasion by all his wives, for the Holy City of Mecca. He started five days before the month began, having put on the pilgrim's dress, and brought victims with him—camels wreathed for the slaughter. A vast multitude followed,

---

[1] Burton says that the term "Greater Pilgrimage" is, in strictness, confined to cases where the chief day (that of sacrifice) falls on a Friday.

and on the tenth day they camped one march from
Mecca. The next morning he entered the city by the
northern gate, and as he rode in he prayed: "O Lord!
increase the dignity and glory, the honour and reverence of Thy House; and greatly increase the honour
and dignity, piety, goodness, and glory of them who
for Pilgrimage (Greater or Lesser) resort thither!" All
the great multitude performed the rites of the Lesser
Pilgrimage, but only those who had brought victims
were allowed to share in the further rites of the
Greater: an exception was made for Ali, who had
joined from his successful expedition to Yaman, and to
whom the Prophet gave a share of his own victims.
On the 7th day of the month he preached to the
multitude at the Kaaba; on the 8th he proceeded to
Minā and prayed; that night he spent in his tent, and
the next morning passed through Muzdalifa to Mount
Arafāt. There he prayed, recited from the Qurān
passages on the rites of Pilgrimage, and concluded:
"This day have I [1] perfected your religion for you, and
fulfilled My mercy upon you, and appointed Islām to
be your religion." Again he spent the night and
prayed in Muzdalifa, and in the morning with many a
loud, "Labbaik!" he hastened to Minā, and cast the
stones at Aqaba. Thereafter he slew his victims,
shaved his head, and pared his nails; the pilgrim's
dress was doffed, the flesh of the victims distributed for
feasting;—and the Great Pilgrimage was at an end.

Three days longer did the Prophet remain at Minā,
and on the second of them he gave a solemn address to
the assembly. He bade them,—"Hearken, for it may
be the last time! Every Muslim is brother to his

[1] Speaking in the name of God.

fellow, and life and property sacred as between you,—
sacred as this month, this land, this Pilgrimage! The
right of inheritance is inalienable! Treat well your
wives, so they be chaste,—for they are as captives and
prisoners to you! Your slaves also ye shall use well!"
He abolished the system of months intercalated, and
restored the reckoning of the year by twelve lunar
months (Q. ix. 37, 38),—a system which has ever since
been the law of Islām.

Then he ended: "Verily, O my people, I have
fulfilled my mission. I have left among you a plain
command,—the Book of God, and manifest ordinances,
the which if ye hold fast ye shall never go astray."
And the people answered, "Yea, verily!" and he
prayed the Lord to bear witness. Then he returned to
Mecca, performed once more the sevenfold circuit,
and drank of the well Zemzem; once more he prayed
in the Holy House; and then after three days he
departed to Medīna. It need scarcely be said that the
Prophet's Pilgrimage is the model which has ever since
been scrupulously followed.

With the return to Medīna began the eleventh year
since the Flight, and Muhammad was now nearly
sixty-three. He had had an arduous life for more
than twenty years, ever since he proclaimed himself
the Apostle of God, and it is no wonder if his iron
frame and constitution were undermined. In April
and May 632 he was busied in issuing despatches,
appointing governors, and arranging the administration
throughout Arabia. The territories of the deceased
Persian governor of Yaman he divided into four provinces. Also there started up to trouble him three
rival pretenders to prophetic power,—Tulaiha in Najd,

Musailima in Yamāma, and Aswad in the south.
Orders were sent out at once to crush them, but could
not be carried into effect before Muhammad had himself passed away. The last warlike expedition which
he planned was a great one against the Roman border,
the special aim of which was to avenge the defeat at
Mūta, when Zaid fell; and the command was given to
Zaid's son, a mere youth,—who was bidden: "Destroy
thy foes utterly: advance speedily and cautiously;
hasten thy march that thy onset may precede tidings
of thee; and tarry not after victory is won." The
camp was formed at Jurf on the 1st Muharram, 27th
May 632, but the army did not start till after the
Prophet was dead. He bound the white banner on its
staff, and gave it to Usāma, saying, "Fight under this
banner in the name of the Lord and for His cause; so
shalt thou break the unbelievers in pieces!"

The end was nigh. In the closing days of May,
Muhammad suffered much from fever, headache, and
weakness. With the consent of all his wives, he took
up his abode with Ayesha, his best-beloved, not yet
twenty years old. The details of his last sickness it is
impossible to ascertain, but it lasted—with intervals of
relief—for about ten days. That he felt his life was
wearing to a close is not doubtful. One day from the
Mosque pulpit he told his people: "Verily, the Lord
hath given the choice to one of His servants, whether
to enjoy a long life here, or to go to meet Him; and he
hath chosen to meet his Lord." No one understood
save Abu Bakr; but he, with the quick understanding
of deep love, at once replied, "May we and our
children be a sacrifice for thee, O Prophet of God!"
And again he said to him one day, "Ah, thou that

art dearer to me than father or mother! alas, grey hairs are hastening upon thee!" And the Prophet answered, "The toil of inspiration! the Suras *Hūd*, and the *Striking,* and their fellows, have made my hair white." One night he rose softly, dressed, and passed out to the graveyard, where rested the "martyrs" of Uhud. For a while he mused; then he blessed and prayed for them, and thanked God that they had reached the promised rest. Then as he went home he told the servant who followed that he himself was soon to share that rest.

The fever was sore on him, and henceforward—until the end came—it left him but seldom. Yet he struggled to fulfil his public duties, led the prayers in the Mosque, and made a special effort to subdue the discontent of the people at the choice of a commander so young as Usāma. But after this he led his people in prayer no more again : Abu Bakr was named to take his place, seeming thus to be marked out as his successor. Special care, too, he showed to recommend to kindly usage the men of Medīna, who had harboured and welcomed him in his need.

On the Saturday his sickness greatly increased; on the Sunday he seems to have been at times unconscious, but he asked for ink and paper to record his last directions,—which for some reason were not brought. Almost his last act was to bid Ayesha give in alms the little store of gold he possessed, and his last words to command that Islām only be allowed in Arabia. On the Monday he rallied so far as to be able to walk feebly to the Mosque, while Abu Bakr led the prayer; but the effort exhausted him, and he came back to lay his weary head on Ayesha's loving breast. His strength sank rapidly, and with broken words of prayer on his lips, and calls to God and to Gabriel, amid the fond, faithful soothing of his young wife, his spirit returned without a struggle to God who gave it.

Ayesha laid his head softly on the pillow, joined her fellow-wives, and gave vent to her grief. The news spread, and reached wise Abu Bakr and fiery Omar,— who both hastened to the house of death. Omar raised the cloth from the face, and then vehemently swore that the Prophet was not dead, " he had but gone like Moses to meet his Lord, and would return." But Abu Bakr followed; and he wept as he gazed on his dead friend, and blessed him with tender words. Then he rebuked Omar, and carried conviction to his heart by quoting the Prophet's own words after the battle of Uhud, as they stand to this day in the Qurān (xxxix. 30, iii. 144): " Verily, thou too shalt die ! Muhammad is no more than an Apostle ; verily, the other Apostles died before him." And he added: "If any man worshippeth Muhammad, Muhammad indeed is dead ; but whoso worshippeth God, let him know that the Lord liveth for ever !"

But public matters claimed their first care. The leaders of the exile went to the great hall of assembly, and there, after brief debate, insisting on the Prophet's oft-repeated word that none could succeed him save a man of the noble clan of Quraish, Omar, the impetuous, clinched the matter by striking the hand of fealty in Abu Bakr's,—and the first Khalifa was elected to rule the thousands of Islām. Then Abu Bakr took up the burden and the trust, and bade the people obey so long as he walked in the Prophet's steps, and slay him if he departed therefrom.

Thereafter they returned to Ayesha's chamber, and, as Muhammad himself had bidden, they laid him to rest where he had died; for that, he had said, was "the ordinance of God for His Prophets." Simple and solemn were the rites: they praised him and thanked God for his mission, and placed him in the grave lying on the red mantle he had been used to wear. In the same chamber were afterwards laid in succession Abu Bakr and Omar; and thither now resort, in reverent throngs, Muslims from every land, as to a place only less holy than the sacred Kaaba itself!

CHAPTER XI

General Review of Muhammad and his System — Personal
Appearance, Habits, and Character—His Teaching—The
Position he claimed for himself—The Qurān—The Future :
Paradise and Hell — Religious and Social Laws — Moral
Duties—Islām and Christianity.

IT is nearly thirteen hundred years since the Prophet
of Arabia died, but the religion which he founded still
rules the hearts and lives of nearly one-sixth of the
human race. To outward appearance Islām is one,
though inwardly it is torn into many sects and schools.
The magnetism of its founder's personality has endured
through all generations, and the short symbol of his
faith has lost none of its power. Yet of him we have
no bust, or statue, or portrait, for such things he
abhorred. To bring before us his outward appearance,
as he moved among men, we turn to the description
collected from the Traditions. "The Prophet was of
middle height, spare and strong, with broad shoulders
and wide chest. A massive, highly-developed head was
covered with dark, thick, slightly curled hair, that fell
to his shoulders. The face was ruddy, the long eye-
brows finely arched, divided by a vein which throbbed
visibly in moments of passion. Black, restless eyes
shone out under long, heavy eyelashes; the nose was
large and aquiline, the teeth well-set and dazzlingly

white, and a full beard framed the face.   He had a clear,
smooth skin, bright complexion, and hands soft as a
woman's.   His step was quick, elastic, firm, 'as one
who steps down from a high place'; in turning he
turned his whole body; and his whole gait and presence were full of dignity.   His countenance was mild
and pensive, and he laughed seldom, but his smile was
very winning.   'Thou wouldst have said, a sun rising.
I saw him at full moon, and he was brighter and more
beautiful than she.'

"In habits he was very simple, but most careful of
his person, especially his teeth.   In eating and drinking,
and in his furniture, he retained his first simplicity;
arms he valued, and rich clothing he sometimes did not
scorn; perfumes he loved, and liquor he hated.   Of a
highly nervous temperament, he shrank from bodily
pain, and would sob and roar under it.   Gifted with
mighty powers of imagination, he had great elevation
of mind, and refined delicacy of feeling.   To his
inferiors he was most indulgent, and scarcely ever
rebuked his servant; to his family he was most affectionate, and he loved all children.   He never cursed,
and his strongest expression was, ' What has come to
him ? may his forehead be darkened with mud !'   He
visited the sick, followed every bier he met, accepted
even a slave's invitation to dinner, mended his own
clothes, waited on himself.   Never was he first to withdraw his hand from another's, nor to turn away ere the
other had turned.   'His hand was the most generous,
his heart the most courageous, his tongue the most
truthful; staunchest was he of protectors, and sweetest
in conversation; and he inspired all men with awe and
reverence.'   He was taciturn of habit, yet playful with

children, but not given to jesting." Such is the picture drawn by the loving pens of disciples, to whom the minutest acts were of importance, and whose highest aim was to follow the Prophet in all things. Palgrave gives a wise caution when he says that the ideals of Arab virtue were first conceived, and then attributed to him. Yet, with every allowance for exaggeration, the man so painted was of very high and noble type. The story of his life shows him to have been of dauntless courage, great generalship, strong love of country; by nature merciful and quick to forgive, there was neither pity nor ruth in his dealings with the Jews, when once he had ceased to hope for their submission. Over and over again he approved assassination, when it furthered his cause; however barbarous or treacherous the means, the end justified it in his eyes; and in more than one case he not only approved, he instigated the foul deeds.

That he was sincere in his effort and desire to reform his countrymen, to raise them from the darkness of their idolatry, to open their eyes to the dread realities of the after-life,—this we cannot doubt. But he took the false, fatal step of proclaiming himself the Apostle of God, specially, continually, exclusively inspired from on high; to support and justify his ambitious schemes, his sensual indulgence, his jealousy, his occasional cruelty and treachery, he feared not to allege the commands of God; to exalt his personal authority he used the Holy Name, on the most trivial, as on the gravest matters; and at length he practically, if not expressly, assumed to abrogate all those previous revelations which in his earlier teaching he acknowledged to be wholly divine. The main outline of his system, with much of its detail, was borrowed from Judaism, and grafted on to the pagan usages of Mecca, yet he professed to have got it all by primary revelation. The great downward step was taken when he fled to Medīna, there to set up his secular kingdom, and when he began the practice of polygamy, after losing his loving and faithful Khadīja.

Before the Flight, Muhammad had only a commission to warn his people, at Medīna he became invested with authority to compel submission and to visit obstinacy with extreme punishment. He was infallible on all matters of faith and conduct, belief in "God and Muhammad the Apostle of God" was absolutely required, "obedience to God and to His Prophet" essential; nay, he delayed his answer to the simplest as to the weightiest questions "till Gabriel should instruct him" of the will of God in the matter. The devotion of his followers during his lifetime was quite boundless, scarcely exceeded by the "worship" now paid to him, as Lane found it in Egypt seventy years ago (M. E. p. 259). What the effect and tendency of his personal example would be on followers who believed that example perfect, any reader of his life may judge.

Muhammad throughout his life always disclaimed the power of working miracles, but his followers have ascribed to him miracles as striking and as varied as those of God's earlier messengers to men. His only "mighty work" was, he said, the Qurān, sent down to him from heaven, perfect beyond human power to rival, an all-sufficient proof and seal of his Apostleship. He claimed also pre-eminence over all other Prophets, in that—as he declared—their messages were to particular peoples or races, but his was "a mercy to all mankind."

The foundation of faith and practice for Muslims are the Qurān, the traditions of what the Prophet commanded or did apart from the Qurān, the consensus of the doctors of Islām, and analogy or deduction from recognised principles in the former sources. The Qurān is the highest authority, the very "Word of God," which the Prophet himself declared to be the all-sufficient guide for his followers. It was not collected till some years after his death, by Zaid, his secretary, under the orders of Abu Bakr, at the suggestion of Omar, and that collection was revised (but with little or no change) under the third Khalifa, Uthmān, and became the authorised version, original copies of which are extant to this day. The substance of the chapters, and their arrangement, rest on Muhammad's own directions. By far the greater part had been set down in writing during his lifetime, much even in the early period of his preaching at Mecca; but the records were dispersed, and gathered together again, as the old report has it, "from date-leaves, and tablets of white stone, and from the hearts of men." The most scrupulous care was exercised, and the universal assent with which the result was accepted is a sufficient guarantee of its faithfulness. But the one hundred and fourteen chapters into which it is divided are arranged entirely without any reference to time of revelation or to subject-matter, but the longest chapters are put first in order. Each chapter begins thus:—"In the name of God, Merciful and Gracious"; a traditional heading states whether the *Sūra* (chapter, "course of masonry") was revealed at Mecca or Medīna, and in

modern editions each Chapter is divided into verses
(āyāt, "signs"), the number of which is stated in the
heading. To twenty-nine of the chapters are prefixed
certain letters, in themselves meaningless, as to the sig-
nificance of which the learned are at a loss. Muslim
doctors give them deep mystic meaning, but Nöldeke's
ingenious guess, that they indicate in some way the
sources from which Zaid collected them, is probably
not far from the truth. The same scholar has also
given us the best arrangement that is now possible of
the Qurān in its chronological order. The whole book
is no longer than two-thirds of the New Testament,
and apart from the long stories of the patriarchs and
former prophets not much longer than the Four Gospels;
yet it is inexpressibly tedious to read through, and—
making every allowance for what is lost in translation
—it is, with some exceptions, immeasurably below the
level of (e.g.) the Psalms or the Book of Isaiah.

The earlier preaching abounds in splendid ascriptions
of praise and glory to God, extolling His boundless,
unutterable majesty and perfections. The people are
warned of the awful consequences that follow after
death on the deeds done in the body; the terrors of
the Judgment-day, when all flesh shall be raised again
to stand their trial before God Almighty, are painted
with awful vividness; and the eternal rest and joy
laid up in store for believers, with the endless woes
reserved for those who reject the Prophet's message,
are set forth in bright and alluring, or in dark and
terrifying hues. But the one satisfying condition for
heaven is acceptance of the Prophet's message, and the
one damning, unpardonable sin, that hurls the soul to
eternal torment, is the rejection of it. The only sin

that God will not forgive is "idolatry," admitting
"partners" to His glory; and as the doctrine is developed it passes specially into reprobation of the
whole Christian dogma. The delights of Muhammad's
Paradise are just such sensual joys as appealed most
strongly to the Arab mind,—peace and rest under
shady trees, with ever-flowing crystal streams, abundance of all manner of dainty food and costly dress,
wine that should cheer the heart but not cloud the
brain, and, above all, dark-eyed virgin brides (Hūris),
"of a rare creation." Faithful women too were to
have their reward in Paradise, but (as Gibbon sneers)
their happiness is left to be imagined. The pains of
hell are similarly described as terrible heat, excruciat-
ing thirst, food and drink of foul and detestable things,
—those miseries which Arabs most dreaded, " that they
may dwell therein for aye," " an evil journey is it " to
" an evil abode."

Very briefly now I shall sketch the outline of the
system of Islām, in its religious, social, and political
working. The five pillars of the Faith are the Creed,
Prayers, Fasting, Almsgiving, and the Pilgrimage.
The foundation-stone (to vary the metaphor) is to
acknowledge, "There is no god but God, and
Muhammad is the Prophet of God." This is the key
to heaven, dying with this on his lips the Muslim
warrior gains the glory of martyrdom, it is the refrain
of all prayer and religious service, and with this the
captive may rescue himself from slavery. And when
the Creed has been accepted, the other duties follow.
First are the five daily prayers at absolutely fixed
times, the first ere the sun rises, and the last shortly
before midnight. The forms of prayer and the postures

are prescribed, and they consist of a limited liturgy from the Qurān, to be repeated in the Arabic tongue, with frequent ejaculation of "God is great!" the Creed, the opening chapter of the Qurān, and other pious formulæ. Prayer must be made looking towards Mecca, and must be preceded by washing, for which in the Traditions the most minute rules are laid down, any breach of which renders the prayer of no effect. Public prayer is made on Friday in the Mosque, and the call from a lofty slender minaret is one of the most attractive formalities of Islām. The crier (Muazzin) chants the call with loud, well-modulated voice, and the faithful who hear it make glad response, and gather to their solemn service. Thus it runs : "God is great! God is great! I witness that there is no god but God (twice)! I witness that Muhammad is the apostle of God (twice)! Come to prayer! Come to prayer! Come to salvation! Come to salvation!" (*at first prayer only*). "Prayer is better than sleep (twice)! God is great! God is great! There is no god but God!" Prayer is led by an Imām, who faces towards Mecca, and the congregation follow him exactly. Only men gather in the Mosque, and Lane (*M.E.* chap. III.) testifies that in Egypt "women seldom pray, even at home." Except for public prayer, Friday is not distinguished from the other days of the week. At the midday service a sermon is also delivered, a homily, of which the chief part is rigidly prescribed, wholly in Arabic, formal and sterile, a large part (obligatory) being taken up with repeated blessings on the Prophet, his family, and the first four Khalifas. Prayers for the dead are also highly meritorious, and of particular efficacy is it to recite or have recited on their behalf the whole of the

Qurān (a *Zikr*). The whole earth, said Muhammad, is
a place of prayer; but prayers in special places—above
all, in his Mosque at Medīna—had an immensely higher
value than elsewhere; and if any prescribed prayer be
omitted, the *same* prayer must be said when it is remembered.

Next in order comes Fasting. This is commended
at all seasons, but commanded only in the month of
Ramadhān. The fast is during the hours of day, from
sunrise to sunset, and is very rigorous; and as the
lunar year makes the month pass through all the
seasons, it presses in hot climates with great severity
on the poor, and it is they who observe it most strictly.
At the end of the fast comes the great Feast-day (*Fitr*,
"breaking," in Egypt *Bairām*), which is celebrated
with the utmost rejoicing. The other great festival of
Islām is that of Azhā, when victims are sacrificed,
borrowed and altered from the Jewish Great Day of
Atonement. It is on this day that the sacrifice is made
in the Greater Pilgrimage.

Almsgiving is highly commended. On the Feast-
day after Ramadhān it is obligatory, but alms are on
that day to be bestowed on the "faithful" only.
Abdul Azīz said, "Prayer carries us half-way to God,
fasting brings us to the door of His palace, and alms
procures us admission."

Pilgrimage to Mecca is a duty incumbent on every
free Muslim of sufficient means and bodily strength
once in his lifetime. The merit of it cannot be obtained by deputy, but it is praiseworthy to send
another on pilgrimage if prevented from going oneself.[1]
The ceremonies are strictly those performed by the

[1] For full details, see Burton's *Pilgrimage*.

Prophet. In modern times, especially in Persia, India, and Afghanistan, pilgrimages are made to the tombs of *Saints*, though such practices were absolutely forbidden by the Prophet.

In family and social relations Muhammad commanded reverence and obedience to parents, and kindness to wives and slaves. The salutation of " Peace," taken from the Jews, is to be given to a fellow-Muslim only. Slander and backbiting are strongly denounced, and even false evidence is allowed to hide a Muslim's fault. Wine, usury, games of chance, are absolutely forbidden, —and not less the making of images or pictures, for " God will at the Resurrection call on their maker to put life in them, and when he cannot, will cast him into hell."   Wives may be taken to the number of four at a time, and may be divorced absolutely at the husband's pleasure, and slave-mistresses are not limited in number. The consequences of this licence need not be dwelt on,—Lane, Burton, Palgrave, and others bear ample witness to it. The seclusion of women is commanded, the husband is expressly allowed to chastise and confine them ; in many cases their evidence is not admitted, and when it is two women's evidence is only worth that of one man ! So long as half the millions of Islām are thus degraded, social progress is impossible, yet the degradation rests on the express commands of the Qurān.

In matters political Islām is a system of despotism at home and of aggression abroad. The Prophet commanded absolute submission to the Imām. In no case was the sword to be raised against him. The rights of non-Muslim subjects are of the vaguest and most limited kind,—and a religious war (Jihād) is a sacred duty whenever there is a chance of success. Hopeless warfare is not enjoined, and it is to this we owe the absence of revolt in India. To the general precept has been due the disastrous wars in the Soudan, the massacres in Crete, in Bulgaria, in Armenia, and the frequent troubles in the north-west border of India. Slavery too is partly a social, and partly a political institution. It has the express sanction of the Prophet, though kindness to slaves is enjoined, and it is praise-worthy to set them free. How the system works in real life let the slave trade of Africa and the savage raids of Turkestan declare!

There is another most important sphere of human life in which the stagnant and fanatical spirit of Islām has wrought incalculable woe, as has in these last days in India been brought into awful prominence. The wise measures of Government to prevent the spread of the dread scourge of plague, especially in crowded cities like Lucknow and Bombay, have been hindered, resisted even to murder of officials, and to a large extent paralysed;—and the reason is, the inviolable seclusion of Muslim women, imposed as a religious duty by Muhammad. We have seen, in former chapters, how jealousy and selfishness lay at the root of this part of the law, to which are sacrificed the lives of thousands, and the happiness of millions throughout the world!

A few words must be said in the end of this chapter as to the relations of Christianity and Islām. Muham-mad's knowledge of Christianity was vague. He imagined that Christians worshipped Christ and the Virgin together with God the Father. Admitting the Incarnation, he denied the Divinity of Our Lord, His Sonship, and the Atonement of His death on the

Cross; indeed, he denied that Jesus had been put to death by the Jews, adopting the heresy that He had been snatched away from their hands and carried up to heaven without dying, and is to come again to restore *Islām* before the consummation of all things. Muhammad also taught that his own message superseded that of Christ, as a more perfect and a final revelation of the will of God. " By their fruits ye shall know them ": Christianity teaches the Fatherhood of God and the brotherhood of all mankind, it has taught mercy and compassion and forbearance for all, and love to all men; it has raised woman to her proper place as the equal of man; and it has established absolute toleration wherever it prevails. Islām is a restricted brotherhood, intolerant of all outside it, degrading and enslaving women. The nations of Christendom, in so far as they follow their Master, constantly advance and extend the cause of mercy, righteousness, peace, and civilisation; but Islām, the more closely it follows the Prophet, the more it stagnates and oppresses, as in Turkey, Morocco, and Persia. Tried by the test of comparison, Islām is a retrogression, not an advance; and the self-styled Prophet, whether himself sincere or not, is condemned by his " fruits " as an impostor; nor will the Christian fail to see that by St. John's test he is the Antichrist, " which denieth the Father and the Son ! "

CHAPTER XII

It is necessary, in order to see how Muhammad's power
continued, and his spirit lived and worked in his first
followers, to trace very briefly the course of events
under his earliest successors, — Abu Bakr, Omar,
Uthmān, and Ali. Of these only the first had a
peaceful end : the others fell, each in his turn, by the
assassin's dagger, a fate that in later ages has overtaken
scores of their successors in all Muslim lands from
Yārkand and Kābul to Constantinople and Morocco.
There is a further reason for this in the fact that the
Qurān, which at Muhammad's death was left scattered
like the Sibyl's oracles, was collected and stamped

with finality under the earlier Khalifas, and that the
great Schism, which has ever since divided Islām into
two hostile camps, hating one another as bitterly as
both hate Christians, was founded under the fourth.
The task of making a brief outline of the history is
lightened by the fact that original authorities are few
and meagre, and have been thoroughly examined and
used by Weil and Muir in their histories of the period.
My own sketch is nothing more than a summary. I
should also caution the reader that, in order to avoid
breaking up the thread of the story, the arrangement
is not always strictly chronological. One domain of
conquest is rounded off before another is taken up.

As has been already told, as soon as Muhammad was
dead, and before he was buried, the chiefs of the
Muslim refugees, with Abu Bakr and Omar at their
head, saw that it was necessary to take immediate
steps to elect as successor a chief whom all parties
would obey. There had always been smouldering
jealousy between the men of Medīna and those of
Mecca. The former had never quite got rid of the
feeling that the latter were strangers and interlopers;
on many occasions Muhammad had shown to his own
townsmen marked favour, the harsh and cruel treatment of the Jews had left rankling memories behind,
and there was a large body still left of those he had
called "Hypocrites," — half-hearted converts, though
these had greatly lost in power since the death of
Abdallah ibn Ubai. So, on a hint from some of their
friends that mischief was afoot, Abu Bakr and Omar
hurried at the head of their followers to the great hall
of Medīna, where already a meeting of citizens was
gathered. The case was critical: if a chief were

11

elected, outside the circle of Muhammad's immediate
friends, it would mean strife and disunion, and perhaps the ruin of Islām.   But the citizens seemed
resolved to choose one of themselves, when Abu Bakr
and Omar appeared, and loudly declared that, honourable and famous though the men of Medīna were,
Arabia would accept as head and leader none save a
member of the tribe of Quraish.—"Then let there be
one chief for us, and one for you." "Nay," was the
statesmanly answer, "there can be but one head." And
the choice was set between Abu Bakr and Omar, when
the latter solved the doubt. "Stretch forth thy hand,"
he said, and struck his own upon it in pledge of fealty.
The rest at once followed his example, citizens as well
as Refugees, and Abu Bakr was elected first Khalifa,
or *successor* to the Prophet.[1]

Abu Bakr was beyond doubt the worthiest and fittest
to succeed his beloved Master. The light of prophecy
had ceased with Muhammad, the new religion was
firmly planted, and the sage, calm, clear spirit of Abu
Bakr was well qualified to deal with the problem of
confirming and extending the infant state. He was a
year or two younger than Muhammad, somewhat short
and spare; his thin face, with high, clear forehead,
sharp, aquiline nose, and deep-set eyes, showed him to
be of the noblest Arab type. His temper was firm but
mild, his faith in his Master absolute and unquestioning; from earliest days he had shared his dangers and
his counsels, and had spent an ample fortune in his
cause. He had been clearly marked out by Muhammad
as his successor, when he was named to lead the Mosque

[1] The title, Commander of the Faithful, familiar in the *Arabian
Nights*, was taken by Omar.

services, and he took up the burden of rule resolutely. In his first address to the people, he said, " O people, I am now your Chief, though not the most worthy.   If I do well, follow me ; if ill, set me right.   Follow after truth, and cast away falsehood.   Even-handed justice will I mete out to you to the uttermost.   Fight stead-fastly in the cause of the Lord.   Obey me as I obey the Lord and His Prophet ; else, obey me not."

In this spirit he acted throughout; his one end was to carry out to the letter every purpose of his Master.

Equally severe to himself and to others in all cases of strict justice, he refused to Fátima the inheritance of some lands which she claimed, but of which she could not prove an absolute destination to her by her father.   There is no ground for believing that Ali at this time pretended to the succession, but there is no doubt that he did not cordially support Abu Bakr, and Fátima's disappointment would intensify his discontent. She, however, survived but a few months, and it is not till after the murder of Omar that Ali showed any open opposition to the Chief of Islam.

When Muhammad was seized by his last illness he had just organised an expedition for war on the Syrian frontier, specially to avenge the reverse at Múta and the death of his faithful Zaid.   The command had been given to Zaid's son Usáma, a young and untried man, and the army lay encamped at Jurf, close to Medína, till after the Prophet's death.   Abu Bakr was urged, but unsuccessfully, either to delay the expedi-tion, in view of the threatening aspect of affairs nearer home, or to entrust the command to some better known leader.   But Usáma went, fulfilled his mission with

brilliant success, and returned after about two months
to Medína.

Abu Bakr had chosen the bold course, and success
justified him. On all sides the tribes were rising in
revolt when he sent away from Medína his only organised army. The desert tribes resisted the tax-gatherers
whom Muhammad had sent out, the whole of Central
Arabia was in open rebellion, and there had sprung up
three rival pretenders to the prophetic office — the
"Veiled Prophet" in Yaman, whose career was cut
short by assassination, Musailima in Yamáma, and
Tulaiha in the north-east. The Khalifa faced all
his foes without quailing. He refused to negotiate,
strengthened Medína as best he could, gallantly repelled
an assault on it, and routed the attacking force. This
turned the tide in his favour, the chiefs who had
hesitated brought in their tithes and made submission,
and Islám was saved !

Arabia had now to be reconquered for the Faith.
Usáma was left in Medína, and Abu Bakr had to carry
out his Master's dying charge, "Throughout Arabia
there shall be no second creed." He himself first
chastised the rebel tribes in battle at Rabaza, con-
fiscated their lands for ever, and then finally returned
to Medína, from which he henceforth directed, without
sharing them, the operations of war and conquest.
The chief "Companions" of the Prophet remained in
Medína with the Khalifa, to share his counsels, and new
men, of whom the chief was Khálid, son of Walíd, led
the armies. He was now sent against Tulaiha, being
a brave and skilful leader, who did incalculable service
to Islám, as formerly he had been its most dreaded foe.
His valour and success earned him the name of the

Sword of God, but his fame is marred by a savage
nature and by cruelty which more than once called
down the censure of Muhammad and Abu Bakr, and at
length ruined him when Omar became Khalifa. As
Khālid advanced, the tribes were overawed and joined
his force, which without much difficulty routed Tulaiha;
whereupon the revolted tribes gave in their submission.
Abu Bakr followed Muhammad in politic clemency,
and pardoned them freely, though he made a few
terrible examples.

Khālid had now a harder task before him. He first
scattered, not without cruelty and bloodshed, the forces
of Mālik, and then passed on his way against Musailima. This man had been in rivalry and collision with
Muhammad himself, with whom he claimed to divide
the Peninsula, as being a Prophet of Allāh equally
with him. The claim was scornfully rejected, and
the claimant dubbed "The Liar." He was a man of
considerable ability, and was enthusiastically supported
by the great Hanīfa tribe and their allies. Attacked
by the Prophetess Sajāh from Mesopotamia, he dis-
armed her by making her his wife, and then bribed her
to go home again to her own land! He had defeated
one Muslim army, and now went to meet Khālid. The
foes met at Aqraba, or Yamāma; a fierce and terrible
battle followed, in which there fell no less than 700
Muslims, among them many of the chief "Companions,"
and a somewhat less number of the enemy; Musailima was slain by the same hand that at Uhud had
laid Hamza low; and victory remained with Khālid.

It was after this great slaughter that Omar strongly
urged the Khalifa to have the Qurān collected and
written down, lest any of the Oracles of God should be

lost. The task was committed to Zaid, Muhammad's
secretary, and the first recension made, and committed
to the charge of Hafsa, daughter of Omar and widow
of Muhammad. This continued to be the authorised
standard till the days of Uthman. It was then found
that discrepancies had arisen, mainly of pronunciation,
and not affecting the substance. A new commission
was appointed, consisting of Zaid and three of the
most learned Quraish; their revision was pronounced
authoritative; all other copies were called in and
burnt; four transcripts were made, and placed in four
of the chief cities of Islām; and the text of the Qurān
then settled has remained unchanged and unquestioned
to the present day. Its correctness is sufficiently
vouched by the fact that no rival interest, whether of
Ali or any other, cast doubt upon it, in spite of ample
opportunity. This recension of the Qurān, though not
perfected in his own reign, and the complete subjugation of Arabia to Islām, were the great achievements of Abu Bakr. Yaman, Hadramaut, and the
provinces that border on the Persian Gulf yielded
to the arms of Ikrima and Khālid, and then the armies
of Islām prepared for conquest beyond their own land,
and the Bedouin hordes flocked to its banner, athirst
for plunder and slaughter.

Accordingly, the beginning of foreign conquest also
falls into Abu Bakr's reign. The first attack was
made upon Persia. Khālid and Muthanna advanced to
the Euphrates, and summoned Hurmuz the Persian
governor to embrace Islām, to submit and pay tribute,
or to stand the attack of a people that "loved death as
he loved life." A battle followed, known to Muslim
history as the "Battle of the Chains," from a story

that part of the Persian army was *chained* together; Hurmuz himself was slain in single fight by Khālid; victory fell to the Arabs, and great and valuable booty rewarded their valour, and stimulated their passions. Victory upon victory followed, though each field was stubbornly contested; at Allis, south of the Euphrates, Khālid celebrated his success by an awful massacre; Hīra accepted tribute and submission, but remained Christian; and a regular Arab protectorate was established. Thus once more the power of Persia was broken, though the end was for a few years delayed; once more her brave but unwieldy hosts failed before her fierce foes, as a thousand years earlier they had failed in the shock of battle at the Granicus and Arbela.

Khālid had next to help to victory his less fortunate namesake in Central Arabia, and then the combined armies swept up the Mediterranean coast, and crowned their triumphs with the capture of Hims and Damascus. The latter did not fall without a desperate resistance, and a great battle was fought almost under its walls; the brave garrison was at last forced to yield; multitudes of citizens, who had escaped before the city fell, were pursued and ruthlessly massacred by Khālid.[1]

Meanwhile Muthanna, left to govern Hīra with a small army, had been hard pressed, and was compelled to seek reinforcements. Abu Bakr prepared to send them, but before they could start the Khalifa was dead, and by his appointment Omar reigned in his stead. Abu Bakr died as he had lived, in simple unquestioning faith and devotion to his beloved Master;

[1] See the awful story as told by Gibbon, chap. li.

he had well and worthily ruled the infant state of Islām, and did it the highest service when he cast the reins of command into the strong hands of Omar. Simple and austere in his life, the rich spoils of Syria and Persia had fallen unvalued into his hands; wisely generous for all public wants, he spent only what was strictly necessary on himself, and died poor, though he had spent an ample fortune for the good of the new Faith. He died on 24th August 634, after a reign of little over two years, and had led the Pilgrimage to Mecca in the spring, following therein exactly the routine which Muhammad had laid down. His last illness was the effect of a chill caught while bathing, and it rapidly took a fatal turn. When he died, he was laid out and buried as simply as the Prophet himself, beside the Master he had loved so well, in the chamber of Ayesha. There, too, the last of the three, was Omar laid when his time came; and it is told of Ayesha that she went thither unveiled so long as only her husband and her father lay there, but that she covered her face when Omar, too, was her silent guest.

Omar's first care was to reinforce Muthanna in Irāq, but at the same time he deposed Khālid from the chief command. Muhammad himself and Abu Bakr had both been alive to the savage and lustful nature of that great warrior; several times they had severely rebuked him, but shrank from punishing him; and it was left for the stern justice of Omar to remove him from the command which his skill and valour had adorned, but which his callous cruelty had so often stained.

After fealty had been sworn to Omar, a large force was sent off under Abu Ubaid to help Muthanna, and that able general hurried back in advance of them to

his government of Irāq. Before the auxiliary army
could reach him, he had won a brilliant victory.   Abu
Ubaid's force met with disaster: a great army was
assembled by the new king of Persia, Rustam, under
the command of Bahmān. Many war elephants marched
with the great host, their huge bulk carrying terror to
the Arab soldiery as, long before, those of Pyrrhus had
to the legionaries of Rome; and the great jewelled
banner of the Persian Empire was unfurled in sign of
the importance of the struggle.   Abu Ubaid, fresh
from his two brilliant victories, prudently withdrew his
comparatively small force of 10,000 men to the right
bank of the Euphrates; but he could not resist a
challenge to cross and give battle on the farther side,
where the nature of the ground hampered his move-
ments. A grave disaster followed. Abu Ubaid himself
was trampled to death by a mighty elephant he had
attacked, the leaders he had named to take his place
fell one after another, and the whole force was in
danger of annihilation through the breaking down of
the bridge of boats. With great difficulty Muthanna,
who had taken command, restored the bridge, and,
though himself severely wounded, drew off the remnant
to the farther side.   Four thousand Muslims had
perished in battle, by drowning, or in flight; two
thousand fled to their homes in Arabia, and the remainder were allowed to withdraw unmolested to Allis,
where Muthanna entrenched himself, as troubles in
Madāin, the capital of Persia, compelled Bahmān to
return there.

Omar received the news of defeat calmly, and comforted the fugitives. Reverse only steeled his purpose,
and nerved him to greater effort.   The victory at

Yarmūk had settled the fate of Syria, and every avail-
able man was sent to Muthanna's aid.   The reinforcements were no sooner come than that great captain,
warned that a strong Persian army was again advancing
to attack him, again marched to the Euphrates to give
battle at Buwaib, not far from where Kūfa was soon to
be built.   He allowed Mahrān, the Persian general, to
lead his whole army across.   Both sides then prepared for battle, and Muthanna heartened his men
with stirring words, and made ready to attack.   The
Persians delivered the first blow, and their fierce onset
for a space threw the Muslims into confusion.   But the
Arab army rallied desperately, and hurled back their
assailants.   The battle raged fiercely; the Persians
were driven back upon the river, and their retreat
being cut off, fought with the courage of despair;
Mahrān fell, and at last victory crowned the Arab
arms.   It was costly but complete, and the booty won
was enormous.   Christian tribes contributed greatly to
the Arab success, and won respect for their religion.
But the jealousy of Jarīr, to which Omar paid too
much respect, robbed Muthanna of the prize he had so
nobly earned; he was superseded in Irāq, which he had
conquered for Islām, and died not long after of the
effects of his wounds.   He was succeeded by Saad, son
of Malik, a relative of the Prophet (he was a nephew of
Khadīja) renowned as he who "shed the first blood
in Islām."   Rapidly advancing, Saad was met by
Muthanna's brother, who brought tidings of his death
and his last counsel, to await the Persian attack on the
west side of the river, with a safe retreat in case of
defeat to the friendly desert.   This advice he followed,
and awaited the reinforcements which were hurrying

to his help from all quarters of Arabia and from Syria.

Rustam came on with a mighty host, under strict orders from the new King of Persia, Yazdagird, to engage the Arabs without delay. The situation bristled with difficulties. The Persian subjects in the invaded territory threatened to join the enemy if they were not protected; on the other hand, the Persian general had hopes that delay might break up the Arab forces, for want of supplies. He was, however, compelled to go forward. By Omar's command envoys were sent to summon the Persian monarch to choose among the alternatives—" Islām, tribute, or the sword"; but they were sent back with scornful words, and the great army went to the decisive battle of Qadīsiya. At the head of 120,000 men, with horse and elephants, he crossed over to engage the enemy, who numbered not much more than one-fourth of his host. Saad himself was prevented by illness from mounting a horse, and this was a discouragement to his men; but his dispositions for the battle were most able, he fired the Arabs with the Prophet's clarion-words on the triumph at Badr, and the signal for attack was the Muslim battle-cry, "Great is the Lord!"

The battle raged for four successive days, and the issue of the first was disheartening to the Muslims. On the second, prodigies of valour were performed, and the balance of advantage was slowly won; the third was marked by the discomfiture of the elephants, which by brilliant and daring attacks were forced back on the Persian hosts, carrying with them confusion and dismay; but on the fourth day Rustam himself was slain, desperate attacks broke the whole Persian line of

battle, and defeat was soon turned into a rout. The
Muslim loss was counted by thousands, but that of the
enemy exceeded it fourfold. The spoil of every kind
taken was enormous, and the blow to the military
power of Persia was fatal. Rapid messengers carried
the great news by relays to Medīna, and the heart of
Omar was made glad with the tidings of victory.

In the following year Saad advanced steadily on
the capital, Madāin, past the world-famous ruins of
Babylon, across the plain of Dura, where long before
the golden image of Nebuchadnezzar was set up. The
tribes, as he advanced, went over to his side, and many
months were spent ere he reached the great capital.
The siege was long and stubborn, for the swift Tigris
formed a natural ditch; but all obstacles were at last
surmounted by the dauntless Arabs, and the capital of
Persia fell. The spoil was rich beyond reckoning or
belief, and the royal gift sent to Medīna filled the
public treasury to overflowing, and made the " Companions" and citizens generally rich. The king of
Persia fled with the remnant of his power to the
mountainous country in the west, and the ritual of
Islām was established in the stately halls of his palace.
The conquest of Eastern Persia was completed some
years later, after another terrible battle at Nahāwand,
when Persia made her final effort to hurl back the
Arab invasion. Yazdagird sought refuge in obscurity,
and the royal line of Persia flickered out.

The victory of Qadīsiya was followed by another at
Jalaula, and then the conquered provinces were settled
by the wise policy of Omar, the native cultivators being
retained on the land, and the great cities of Kūfa and
Basra (Bussorah) founded for the Arab conquerors, who

settled there in large numbers. Kūfa was founded
near Hīra, the ancient capital of the old Christian
principality, and became, in place of Madāin, the seat of
government for Persia; Basra, at the head of the
Persian Gulf, became ere long a great seat of commerce.
Not very willingly did Omar give leave for the building of cities for the conquering Arabs; he commanded
that all dwellings should be simple, and he compelled
Saad himself to pull down the gateway he had
built before his palace. Both the new cities were
amply dowered from the tribute of the country around;
they grew rapidly in wealth and importance, and their
rivalries and factions were fatal to the best interests of
Islām.

While Saad had been warring in the east, Abu
Ubaid and Khālid had reduced Syria and Palestine;
after that, Amru conquered the rich land of Egypt,
which became for Arabia—what it had been for the
Roman Empire—the great granary; and last of all the
conquest of Persia was completed. Thus when Omar
died there had been added to the domain of Islām
Egypt and Syria, Palestine and the whole land of
Persia; nor was the Muslim power in that vast tract of
country again seriously disturbed till the time of the
Crusades, when, at intervals, for the space of two
centuries, the warriors of Christendom strove, but in
vain, to wrest from infidel hands the cradle of our
faith.

After Damascus had fallen, the Arab forces, ably led
by Abu Ubaid and Khālid, gradually defeated and
wore down in many hard-fought fields the armies of
Heraclius. One stronghold after another yielded to
siege and assault, and at length the Emperor himself

in despair withdrew across the Bosphorus, abandoning
the fair Asiatic provinces of his empire, after well-nigh
seven centuries of Roman rule.   From the coast-lands
of Syria Amru turned his arms against the Roman
general, Artabūn, won a great and bloody victory at
Ajnadain, and laid siege to Jerusalem, a city scarcely
less holy in Muslim than in Christian or Jewish eyes.
The Patriarch was forced to treat, but stipulated to
deliver up the city only to the Khalifa in person.   On
receiving the message, Omar at once set out, travelled
with the utmost speed and simplicity, " mounted on a
red camel," which carried his provision of dates and
water, sharply rebuked the luxury and state of the
commander who came to meet him, and received with
noble clemency the surrender of the Holy City.   He
showed much delicacy and consideration, both for
Patriarch and people, laid the foundation of the mosque
which to this day bears his name, and returned with as
little state as he came.

In the following year (638 A.D.) a last great effort
was made to shake off the Arab yoke in Northern
Syria, but it ended only in the more complete subjugation of the country.   But the close of the conquest
brought also the downfall of Khālid, who had had the
chief share in it.   Accused of luxury and malversation,
he was summoned by Omar to Medīna, and there he
was degraded, stripped of his wealth, and left to die
some years after in penury and neglect.   There seems
justice in his bitter complaint that the Khalifa had
used him till he needed him no more, and then punished
him, in reality for offences long since condoned ; but it
may be that fuller knowledge would quite clear Omar
of the stain of ingratitude.

The third and last great field of conquest in Omar's reign was Egypt. Lying contiguous on its north-eastern borders with the peninsula of Sinai, to which the Prophet himself had led an expedition; famous in Arab history and sacred legend; renowned through all time for riches, learning, and fertility,—it offered temptation irresistible to the ambition of Amru, the great general who had in a few years subdued Palestine and Syria. Not without difficulty he got from his cautious and unaggressive master leave to attempt the conquest. Church feuds, only more bitter as they less concerned the essentials of religion, had made the people ill-disposed to their Byzantine rulers, while ruthless taxation drove them to despair. The occasion was favourable to the invaders, especially as they had so often overcome the best armies of the Empire. Amru therefore advanced from Palestine by the easternmost branch of the Nile, in the end of 640 A.D. After several minor victories, in one of which fell Artabūn, his old opponent in Syria, he captured Memphis, or Misr, and gave terms to the city and its governor Maqauqas, who in years gone by had sent to Muhammad Mary the Copt and her sister. He then moved down to Alexandria, and without much difficulty reduced that important city and seaport also; then, returning by Omar's command to Upper Egypt, he founded the camp-city of Fustāt, which soon extended and grew into imperial Cairo, the chief glory of which is to this day Amru's splendid mosque. The conqueror followed his master's wise policy, confirmed the native cultivators on the land, and reopened the old navigable canal that connected the Nile with the Red Sea, whereby former work of ancient Pharaohs was made to serve the needs of Arabia. Again the cautious moderation of the Khalifa checked the ambition of his lieutenants, and for long Alexandria was used only for defence, and not for attack on the Roman Empire. Once established in Egypt, however, Islām had taken the first step in that great westerly advance which was not checked before the great victory of Tours, a hundred years later, and its dominion still lasts over the whole north littoral of Africa, where once were some of the most famous homes of Christianity.

The rule of Omar was not less successful at home than abroad. As already noticed, the first collection of the Qurān, begun under Abu Bakr, was completed in his time, and the manuscript committed to the custody of his daughter Hafsa. Following out what he believed to be the Prophet's wish, if not his direct command, he drove from their homes in Arabia, but not without fitting compensation, all Jewish and Christian tribes who would not embrace Islām. Beyond Arabia, however, his dealings with both these religions were marked by so much mercy and fairness, that we can have little doubt that his action within Arabia was dictated by motives of sound policy. Arabia was to be the stronghold and recruiting-ground for the armies of Islām, tribal jealousies were hard enough to deal with, and he felt that it was indispensable that the bond of religion should be unbroken. Muslim tradition attributes to his "Code" a whole system of severe and degrading tyranny, with just as little ground as Roman orators referred later legal doctrines to the Laws of Numa.

In pursuance of his plan to keep the Arabs a race apart, a warrior people, they were all carefully num-

bered, registered, and classed. Priority in the faith,
martial descent, and spiritual eminence alone gave rank
in the brotherhood of Islām, and the various pensions
(which were hereditary) were allowed from the vast
spoils of their rich conquests,—ranging from the large
sums given to the "Mothers of the Faithful"
(Muhammad's widows) to the small allowances of the
rank and file.

The year 639 A.D., the fifth of his reign, is known as
the "Year of Ashes," when for nine months plague
and famine desolated Arabia and the neighbouring
countries. When the trial was past, the Khalifa
journeyed through Syria to settle the administration,
and replaced Abu Ubaid, carried off by the plague, by
Muāwiya, the son of Abu Sufiyān, an able, resolute,
unscrupulous man, which choice afterwards caused
the first split in Islām. Omar regularly led the
Pilgrimage to Mecca, and at one of his visits he laid
out the great square round the Kaaba, where now is
the many-colonnaded House of Prayer.[1] He also fixed
the Muhammadan era of the Hijra, beginning from
the 1st of Maharram 622 A.D., the year being, by
Muhammad's command at the Farewell Pilgrimage,
reckoned as of twelve *lunar* months. He was a ruler
of stainless integrity, great courage, and unflinching
resolve, and his justice is proverbial. Zealous, even to
the death, for the laws of his Master, he time after time
removed and degraded his highest officers for trivial
infractions of the law. Khālid, and Saad, and Mughīra
felt the lash of his anger ; yet riches and luxury combined with the unnatural restraints of Muhammad's
law to sap the foundations of morality, and it is from

[1] For a minute description, see Burton's *Pilgrimage*.

12

Omar's reign that dates the decadence of Muslim social life. A multitude of slaves, and a plethora of wealth cast the conquering race into the lap of luxury; debarred from wine, games of chance, and other relaxations natural to man, with unbounded choice within the harem, to which their women were confined, the degradation of both sexes could not fail to advance with fatal rapidity. Drunkenness and every kind of debauchery defied even the strong hand of Omar to restrain them, and he himself fell by the hand of a murderer, a Persian slave, who stabbed him in the great Mosque of Medīna, as he opened the solemn service. He died firm in the Faith, leaving behind him a great name, the fame of a wise ruler, and the empire of Islām firmly established. The Shias, who abominate the first three successors of the Prophet, are peculiarly bitter against the memory of Omar, because (no doubt) of his unquestioned greatness. Burton also is less than just to him, and calls him " little better than a self-righteous formalist," while in his eyes Ali is the "first man of genius to wear the Prophet's mantle."

CHAPTER XIII

ABU BAKR and Omar had each given a daughter in
marriage to the Prophet, and the next two Khalifas
were his sons-in-law. As we have seen, Omar had been
named to the succession by Abu Bakr on his deathbed,
and now the choice was left by him to five electors, of
whom every one (save only his son Abdul Rahmān)
aspired to the office. Omar had solemnly warned them
all against ambition and self-seeking, but that did not
prevent jealousy and intrigue; and at length, on the
day limited by him, Uthmān was proclaimed successor.
Ali resented the choice, but took the oath of allegiance;
and thenceforward there were two parties in Islām.
The policy, pursued by both former Khalifas and continued by Uthmān, of keeping in Medīna, as a sort of

standing council, the chief Companions, instead of em-
ploying their energies in war and foreign conquest,
was hazardous, and was now to bear bitter fruit.
Even the strong, self-reliant Omar had more than once
unwisely yielded to popular clamour. Uthmān was
naturally weak, yet obstinate, and had never had the
same commanding place and influence with Prophet
and people as the first two Khalifas, though personally
he had been a favourite with Muhammad. Besides, he
was now old, and had to reckon with personal envy
and ambitions which had sprung up with the expansion of Islām. Omar had lost a powerful chief from
his side by insisting on a poor Bedouin's right of
retaliation, while Uthmān's first act was to refuse to
execute justice on a murderer. In the light of what
followed, it is strange to find Ali insisting on punishment. The son of Omar, misled by a false report, that
the assassin of his father had just before the murder
been seen in close conference with a Persian slave and
with the Persian prince Harmuzān, slew them both.
There was no evidence against them whatever, and the
murder of the prince, who was a convert to Islām, demanded the penalty of death. Uthmān, however,
shared the general feeling of horror that father and
son should be cut off as in one day; so he remitted the
penalty of death, and compelled the relatives to accept
the bloodwit. But though this act was in harmony
with the people's will, much else in his life and reign
was far otherwise. In particular he alienated their
sympathies by advancing and favouring his own relatives, yielding at times unreasonably to popular
clamour, yet showing in other matters petulant
obstinacy,—as when he changed and added to some

of the ceremonies of the annual Pilgrimage to Mecca, and would give no reason for his action other than that such was his pleasure. He changed, and changed more than once, every one of the able lieutenants of Islām, save only Muāwiya, who was a relative of his own, and Muāwiya proved a firm friend and support to him so long as he lived, and strove to the utmost to avenge his murder.

The first cause of Uthmān's failure as a ruler will be found in his age. When he succeeded Omar he was already past seventy, and he came in the stead of a man nearly twenty years younger, a man of singular vigour both of mind and body. The problems of empire had grown with startling rapidity in the ten years of Omar's reign, and even he had not been at all times equal to them; far less was his successor. Omar had always been ready to take the field, and had shrunk from no toil or personal hardship in the interests of his people, nor would he brook the least breach of his commands, or of the law of Islām; inflexibly just, yet without a trace of cruelty, his ablest and strongest lieutenants stood in awe of him, and laid down honours and commands at his bidding. When he fell, all was changed. The years that had elapsed since last Medīna was threatened, just after the Prophet's death, had done much to enervate the citizens, and the Companions of Muhammad, men of renown for war and counsel in his days, had—through long inaction—the " native hue of resolution sicklied o'er." There were besides two special causes of division in the kingdom, the rivalry of the Quraish with the rest of the Arabs, and that of the family of the Prophet (the " sons of Hāshim "), now represented

by Ali and his sons, and that of Umaiya, to which
Uthmān belonged.   At the head of the former party
was Ali, whose skill and bravery had lain inactive
since the Prophet's death, and who had sunk into the
dangerous luxury of the harem; naturally ambitious,
we cannot doubt that he chafed at his inaction.   As
time went on, he was encouraged by the general discontent, he could not forget that he had only just
missed the succession; and he was flattered by the
high claims put forward on his behalf by preachers of
sedition, who urged a divine right of succession in-
herent in the Prophet's family, of which he was the
head.   Moreover, among Uthmān's bitterest enemies
were sons of his predecessors; and the dangerous
elements in Kūfa and Basra increased the difficulties
of his task; Kūfa, in addition, was jealous of the
Syrian province,—so that strife broke out when reinforcements had to be sent from the west to complete
the conquest of Persia, delayed both by insurrection
and by Turkomand invasion.

In Egypt the Khalifa won through his lieutenants
brilliant successes, but the displacing of Amru by
Abu Sarh, his own foster-brother and, at one time,
Muhammad's secretary, was most unpopular.   Even
the conquests in North Africa, the reduction of
Cyprus, and a great naval victory over the Byzantines,
did not allay the discontent.   In Kūfa matters went
from bad to worse.   Saad had been replaced in office
immediately after Omar's death; but he ruined himself
by extravagance, and his successor—Walid, son of
Uqba, one of the prisoners massacred after Badr, had
to be deposed, recalled, and scourged for flagrant
drunkenness.   Similarly, at Basra, Uthmān unfor-

tunately replaced Abu Mūsa, who had fallen a victim
to faction, by a young cousin of his own ; and this
man increased his master's unpopularity by filling all
offices with his own relatives. Another young kinsman,
Saīd, was appointed to rule Kūfa, a man whose father
had also fallen at Badr fighting against the Prophet.

All these matters combined to rouse hostility against
Uthmān, and to their fire fuel was added by his
action in regard to the Qurān. The recension, not
long completed under Omar, had suffered corruption as
it was copied and went through the various provinces
of the empire ; moreover, differences of pronunciation
had arisen, and all variations from right reading of the
very "Word of God" was deadly sin. Accordingly,
variants were called in, the true text reconstituted by
a commission of the Quraish on a comparison with the
original in Hafsa's care ; authentic copies were made
of the revised text, and distributed as archetypes ; and
all others were called in and burnt. On this was
founded by the malcontents (especially at Kūfa) a
charge of sacrilege against Uthmān. It mattered
little that there was no foundation for the charge, it
was equally fatal. Again, he stirred hostility in carrying out at Mecca that enlargement of the Kaaba square
which Omar had begun ; and by making of his own
mere will certain changes in that ritual of the Pilgrimage which was sanctified by Muhammad's example.
To this was added the loss, trifling in itself, of the
Prophet's signet-ring, which fell from his finger into
a freshly-dug well : and now the accumulated forces
of disloyal faction were ready to overwhelm him.

There arose a Jewish convert who preached the
doctrine of Ali's divine right, and of the "second

coming" of Muhammad himself. The poisonous leaven worked, and along with it came sedition in Kūfa, to which the Khalifa yielded, with results fatal to himself. The governor was driven out, and retired to Medīna; emissaries of rebellion moved and plotted throughout the empire; hesitating measures of repression only made things worse; and Uthmān shrank from the stern courses which alone could avail. Ali, as spokesman of the people, remonstrated, but gave neither support nor practical advice; and a despairing appeal to the people also brought neither help nor counsel. Even in Medīna insult was poured on the Khalifa as he passed through the streets, and seditious cries assailed his ears. A commission was sent out to inquire into causes of discontent and possible remedies, but was fruitless of good; the governors of provinces were summoned to Medīna to advise their sovereign, but only Muāwiya gave counsel of weight,—either to go with him to Egypt or to receive into Medīna a commanding Egyptian force. But both proposals were rejected, the faithful viceroy went his way after solemn warning to Ali and the other chiefs, and the final catastrophe hurried on.

Conspirators gathered from Egypt, from Kūfa, and from Basra, having among their leaders Muhammad, son of Abu Bakr and brother of Ayesha. They marched on Medīna, on pretence of visiting the Prophet's Mosque and tomb, and were at first baffled in their attempt to enter the city; but succeeded by a stratagem. They rudely called on Uthmān to abdicate, "for the Lord had cast him off," and on his refusal, rejecting all promises of reform, they threatened him with death. Strife and tumult reigned in Medīna;

Ali and the other chief men gave no real help; for many weeks the Khalifa was blockaded, till at length the final assault was made, and the defences broken down, before troops sent by Muāwiya to the rescue could reach their goal. Uthmān was murdered as he sat in an inner chamber reading the Qurān, and was buried hastily with maimed rites, amid a shower of stones and curses from his murderers. Thus, after a troubled reign of twelve years, died Uthmān, too weak to take up Omar's sceptre, too pitiful to use that sword which alone might have saved him.

Uthmān was dead, the second prince over Islām to fall beneath the murderer's dagger. As Omar had been stabbed at the entering in of the Mosque, so had Uthmān been slain as he read aloud from the Sacred Book, as tradition tells that the Prophet had foretold of him; and it is added, that his blood flowed down the page to the words (S. ii. 138), " If they rebel, verily they are in schism, and God will suffice thee against them." Those who had fought for him to the last now scattered, and his blood-stained shirt and the severed fingers of his faithful wife Nāila (wounded in his defence) were swiftly borne away to Muāwiya in Syria, to cry aloud for vengeance, and by Muāwiya's command were hung up in the great Mosque at Damascus.

The murderers held sway in Medīna; for a few days anarchy reigned; and then Ali was, by their ill-omened power compelling the citizens, raised to the throne. He may well have shrunk from the heavy task before him. He was no longer the fiery dauntless Ali, who had sprung to his feet to " bear the burden" for the Prophet, the very Peter of Islām. At the death of

Muhammad he was a man (probably) of about forty, an able and valiant warrior, and of sound, sober judgment. Thrice passed over in the succession, he was now quite as old as the Prophet had been when he died, and had lost his early fire and decision, retaining only that softness of character which was to prove his ruin, as it had been Uthmān's. His one chance of mastering the forces now rising against him lay in quick, stern, unsparing resolve. But his action during the last years of Uthmān, due (we cannot doubt) largely to the enervating luxury of his large harem, showed he was not able to cope with his difficulties.

Twelve years before he had insisted that Omar's own son should be put to death for murder, but now he took no steps to punish the murderers of Uthmān, traitors and rebels as well. Thus he was untrue to himself, he put weapons into the hands of his enemies, and he alienated the support of those who might have been powerful friends—Muāwiya and Ayesha. The latter had probably never liked Ali, she was suspected of having stirred up enmity against Uthmān, but at the last she had thrown all her influence on his side, and she was shocked and grieved at his fate, not least because her own brother Muhammad was a ringleader in the crime. She heard the news on her way back from the Pilgrimage to Mecca, and returned thither vowing vengeance on the murderers. Ere long she was joined by Zubair and Talha, mighty men of renown, who had sworn allegiance to Ali, but recanted on the plea of compulsion.

Ali meanwhile shrank from pursuing the murderers, but rashly persisted against all faithful counsel in deposing all the chief lieutenants of the empire.

Especially did he commit a fatal blunder in attempting to depose Muāwiya, before he was strong enough to enforce his will. That great viceroy was firmly fixed in the affections of his subjects, in Syria was settled a strong, orderly and well-disciplined host of the best Arab stock, and Abu Sufiyān's son was himself more than a match for Ali. He defied him, and sent him word that Syria was to a man resolved to avenge Uthmān's murder on him.

Ali's call to arms was but ill answered. His first task was to meet the rebels who, led by Talha and Zubair and accompanied by Ayesha, had marched upon Basra, seized the city, put to death many of the rebels against Uthmān, and were stirring up revolt in Kūfa and elsewhere. To Kūfa he marched, gathering strength by the way, and being again strongly aided from the city, led his now large army against Basra. Negotiations were wrecked by Bedouin treachery, and a fierce and bloody battle followed, that of the "Camel," so named from that which Ayesha rode, and from which she urged on the fight. Ali was the victor, his two chief opponents fell, and Ayesha, round whose camel the fiercest fighting had taken place, was made prisoner. Her Ali treated with most chivalrous courtesy, and dismissed her safe under escort. She went first to Mecca, and then finally retired to Medīna, where she lived for more than twenty years longer, dying at the age of about sixty-six. The traditions of the Prophet traced back to her are very numerous, and doubtless she knew more of him and his thoughts and ways than did any other.

In January 657 (A.H. 36) Ali entered Kūfa, which was thenceforward his capital. His next encounter must be with Muāwiya, and both leaders prepared for the contest. Partly by force, partly by fraud, Ali's viceroy was ousted from Egypt, and replaced by Amru, who made close alliance with Muāwiya. One more effort Ali made to avoid hostilities, sending an envoy to invite Muāwiya to swear allegiance; but, in answer, again the condition was made that the regicides must first be punished. This unhappily was beyond Ali's power, so he gathered a great host of 50,000 men, and went forth to attack his foe. He followed the course of the Euphrates upwards, to a point nearly due east of Antioch, crossed the river at Riqqa, not without a good deal of opposition, and met the enemy at Siffīn. Muāwiya had a force at his command superior in number, equal in valour and devotion, and far better disciplined. Negotiation was tried in vain; Ali could not take the bold, and only safe, course of denouncing and punishing the murderers of Uthmān, and there was no other common ground on which Muāwiya and he could meet. Desultory fighting, with truces in between, went on from May to July 637; in the hottest hours of the battle, Ali showed all his ancient valour, and the victory was snatched from him by craft. At Amru's suggestion, Muāwiya caused the Qurān to be raised aloft as a standard; the battle was stayed; both parties, after long conference, agreed to trust the cause to decision of arbitrators,—Amru for Muāwiya and Abu Mūsa for Ali, that so (if it might be) divisions might be healed, and peace restored to Islām. The decision was to be given after six months, at some neutral spot between Kūfa and Damascus, and the rivals retired each to his own capital. The slaughter on both sides had been great, mourning reigned throughout the whole land, an arbitrator beneath his task had been forced by faction on Ali, who had been driven to appear as champion of regicides, and the whole balance of gain lay with his wily foe.

Fresh trouble sprang up for Ali as he marched homewards. Appeal to the Qurān meant for the Bedouins, whose real revolt was against Quraish ascendency, freedom and equality among all Muslims. Twelve thousand of Ali's troops accordingly hived off from him, declared for pure theocracy, and were only pacified for a time by Ali declaring for the same principles.

In February 658 (Ramadhān 37 A.D.) the umpires met at Duma, half-way between the rival capitals, each with an escort of 400 men. After brief conference they agreed to depose both the rivals, and then to leave a free choice to the people. Abu Mūsa, Ali's umpire, pronounced the decision, and then Amru confirmed Ali's deposition, but confirmed Muāwiya as Khalifa.

The decision was at once adopted in Syria, and Muāwiya proclaimed; and in Kūfa it was as heartily denounced; the rival heads of Islām cursed one another in solemn services as fervently as did Pope and Antipope in later days; and the flames of civil war were kindled afresh.

But before he could attack Muāwiya, Ali had to deal with the theocratic Separatists, who raised, without delay, the standard of rebellion, and drew off to Nahrwān, to the north beyond Baghdad. A general levy was made to march against Syria, but the rebels had first to be crushed. Ali gained more than one bloody victory over them, and then led his army

against Syria.   But the fickle, half-hearted troops fell
gradually away, and the march was abandoned ; while,
to add to Ali's losses, Egypt also was gained over to
the enemy, and Muhammad, son of Abu Bakr, was
slain.   Broken in spirit, weighed down by trouble and
disloyalty, Ali had once and again to quell Separatist
revolts.   Mecca itself was trampled under foot, first by
Muāwiya's forces and then by Ali's, and Arabia was
torn with civil war.   The internecine strife lasted for a
year or two, and then, in 660 A.D., Ali and Muāwiya
made peace.   But in the next year some fanatics
banded themselves together to assassinate simultane-
ously Ali, Muāwiya, and Amru ; Ali fell, as he entered
the Mosque, beneath a poisoned blade, and died in a
short time, leaving to his sons, Hasan and Husain, a
heritage of trouble.   So died the Lion of Islām, the
Prophet's well-loved cousin and son-in-law ; brave,
generous, single-hearted, too simple for his adversaries,
not stern enough for his time.

On the death of Ali, Hasan, his eldest son, was
elected at Kūfa to succeed him, for Ali had refused to
nominate a successor ; but he was a mere voluptuary ;
and when Muāwiya with a formidable army came to
attack him, he, after a feeble show of resistance,
abdicated, and retired to Medīna, with a liberal pen-
sion from the conqueror.   There he indulged those
sensual tastes which earned him the name of " The
Divorcer," and after eight years of this ignoble life
was poisoned by one of his wives.   The story which
lays the guilt of this crime on Muāwiya may be dismissed as a calumny.   He entered Kūfa as a conqueror,
made himself master of the whole Muslim Empire, and
for many years more reigned in peace at Damascus.

He created much scandal by acknowledging as his brother Ziyād, who was the offspring of vagrant love on his father's part, but the act undoubtedly strengthened his throne. To provide against a recurrence of civil war at his death, he chose his son Yazīd to succeed him, and required, during his lifetime, an oath of allegiance to his nominee. In the conquered provinces this was obtained without difficulty, but force was required to impose the condition on the Holy Cities, and at Mecca the end was only reached by threats of the sword. At length, in April 680, Muāwiya died, being nearly eighty years old, and Yazīd reigned in his stead.

As Muāwiya had warned him, Yazīd soon found a pretender spring up in Husain, second son of Fātima and Ali. He escaped from Medina to Mecca, to avoid the oath of allegiance, and was then tempted by urgent promises and invitations to start for Kūfa, in the dangerous part of pretender. His best friends warned him against trusting the Kūfans, but in vain; so he set out with all his family and friends, and a small bodyguard of thirty devoted adherents.

But Yazīd was on the alert, and sent an able, unscrupulous governor, Ubaid Allah, son of Ziyād, to master the rebellious city. Husain's messengers, sent to feel the public pulse, were seized and put to death; the Kūfans dared not rise; and the governor sent a strong troop of horse to bar Husain's passage, to demand his unconditional surrender, and to prevent his return to the Hijāz. The Arab tribes that had been flocking to his side, seeing now small chance of success, melted away from him; he pleaded in vain to be allowed to surrender, on promise of being sent before Yazīd at Damascus;

and at length, hemmed in by his foes and cut off from
the river, his only water-supply, Husain and his small
faithful band were attacked and annihilated on the fatal
field of Karbalā.   One after another, selling their lives
dearly and slaying more than their own number of the
enemy, sons, nephews, brothers, cousins of Husain fell
beneath the swords and the arrows of the Kūfan
soldiery ; the little camp was ravaged with fire also,
from the burning reeds of the river-bank ;—last of all
fell Husain himself, and the cavalry rode over the
corpses.   All the fighting men were slain, and their
heads, seventy in number, carried,—a ghastly load,—
along with the captive women and children, to the feet
of Ubaid Allah, Yazīd's savage representative.   Muāwiya's last charge to his son had been to "deal gently
with Husain, for verily the Prophet's blood courses
through his veins."   But the governor roughly turned
the bloody head over with his staff, to the horror of his
own courtiers, and an aged man rebuked him with the
words, "Gently, for it is the Prophet's grandson.   By
the Lord ! I have seen these very lips kissed by the
blessed mouth of Muhammad !"

A sister, two little sons, and two daughters, alone
were left now of the Prophet's descendants.   These were
sent first to Damascus, and thence after a time, with all
honour and respect, to the deserted homes in Medīna.
The tragedy of Karbalā took place on the 10th of
Muharram 61 A.H., and that day has since, through
many centuries, been observed with the deepest grief
and wildest and most enthusiastic devotion by the
followers of the great *Shia* schism, the universal
creed of Persia and the lands which Persia influenced.
Seventy years later the memory of Karbalā hurled the

Umayyads from the throne; to this day it is for millions
of Muslims a shrine as holy as Mecca or Medīna, and
the death-caravan pursues evermore its mournful way
through the deserts of Persia, to lay the faithful dead
to rest in the soil hallowed by Husain's bones. From
the feeble remnant of Ali's family have sprung, in
later centuries, countless thousands of Sayyids, the
aristocracy of birth in Islām.

Thus was for ever extinguished the secular power in
the Prophet's own family; for the Abbāsids represented
his uncle. Karbalā was fought sixty, and Ali was
murdered forty, years after the Flight. Taking the
commonly received dates of the first Christian century,
the murder of Ali would correspond in time (dating from
our Lord's baptism) with the martyrdom of Peter and
Paul, and the massacre at Karbalā with that of St. John.
In the one case the "blood of the martyrs was the seed
of the Church," faithful to her Lord's word, that "His
kingdom was not of this world"; the Prophet of Arabia,
on the contrary, claimed this world as his kingdom, and
his servants fought for him, and have long prevailed;
the choice of "Islām, tribute, or the sword," solemnly
pronounced by himself, and offered in his own day by
his lieutenants, has been the rule of his Empire ever
since. The martyrs of Islām are her warriors slain on
the battlefield, fighting the enemies of their Prophet,
generally in aggressive warfare, not those who are
haled before kings and rulers for the Master's sake, and
who shed their blood for faith in His name.

CHAPTER XIV

The Qurān—Its Composition, Literary Character, and Influence—
Fixes the Arabic Tongue—Not collected by Muhammad—The
Fātiha—The Doctrine of Allāh, with Extracts—Man's relation
to God : his Moral and Religious Duties, Future Life, and
Rewards and Punishments—The Higher Law of Christ—
Creation and Providence—The Resurrection—Paradise and
Hell—Illustrative Extracts—Muhammad's Debt to Judaism—
His Inferiority—Women in Islām—Slavery.

THE paradox has been maintained [1] that Christianity
would be a force quite as great in the world without the
Old and New Testaments as with them.   Not many will
be found to admit this ; but, however it might be with
Christianity, it is quite certain that the existence of
Islām is bound up with the Qurān.   Were it for nothing
else, the whole fabric of religious observances rests
upon it.   The daily prayers, the Friday general service,
all solemn affairs to which the sanction of religion is
attached, the wedding and the burying of the " faithful,"
and the memorial services for the good of their souls,—
all are founded on the Qurān, and have no existence
save through it.   Apart from this, however, looked
upon merely as literature, the service to his people and
tongue which Muhammad did by composing the Qurān

[1] Among others, a distinguished Edinburgh Advocate and well-
known adherent of the United Free Church of Scotland, has urged this
view.

194

is altogether beyond estimate. Before him there existed
nothing in Arabic but poetry, fragmentary songs and
ballads, which indeed show the language highly developed, with all the qualities needed for making a great
literature. But prose was not yet in existence, little
was recorded in writing, and divergent dialects threatened to prevent the formation of a national tongue.
Muhammad gave Arabia the first prose she possessed,
the sacred character of the Qurān fixed for ever the type
of language that should prevail,—the cultivated dialect
of the Quraish, and the balanced rhythm of the Prophetic oracles, modified from ancient Arab poetic form,
and comparable with the parallelism of Hebrew poetry,
permeates all later Arabic literature. Without an ex-
tensive and accurate knowledge of the Qurān, countless
allusions and phrases are unintelligible; every good
Muslim has by heart many chapters from its sacred
pages, and repeats not a few in his daily prayers; and
the title *Ḥāfiz*, highly prized, and known to the West
chiefly as the poetic name of the sweetest mystical
bard of Persia, signifies one who can repeat the
whole Book from end to end. Luther created modern
High German by his translation of the Bible; our
own Authorised Version has given permanency and
high excellence to the English language, forming a
bond imperishable for the Anglo-Saxon race; but
in both Germany and England there existed already
a great and vigorous literature, so that the service
which Muhammad rendered to his people was even
greater.

The peculiar feature of the Semitic group of languages, the tri-consonantal radicals, whose primary development by vowels gives the *verb*, with its almost

endless variety of inflection, and the substantive forms
springing from them, induces a similarity of word-
endings which makes it (in Burton's phrase) "almost as
difficult *not* to rhyme in Arabic as in Italian." From
this comes the peculiar system of Arab rhyme, a whole
long poem having every line ending in the same sound,
and even with a double assonance. One and the same
succession of vocalised syllables, filling up the tri-consonantal skeleton, or amplifying it by (so-called) *servile*,
or formative, additions, gives the same or similar modifi-
cation of the primary sense of the radical; and thus
form and sense and sound suggest and harmonise with
one another. Naturally these things were a help to the
memory, just as the metrical form of the oldest Aryan
literature, Vedic and Orphic Hymns, or the Laws of the
Twelve Tables, made it more easy to keep them in memory. Muhammad heartily abhorred poets and poetry,
and vehemently denied the imputation that he himself
was a poet; yet his earliest revelations have much of the
spirit, and not a little of the form, of poetry. It is this
which gave power to his message, though his bold
challenge to "produce a chapter like unto them, if they
be not verily the Word of God," depended (as Nöldeke
remarks) as much on the substance as on the language
and form. Anyone who had repeated Muhammad's
message would have stood convicted of imitation, and
a copy is ever far below the original. The first
Meccan Sūras come hot from the heart, it is they which
(he said) had turned his hair grey; and later the eloquence might, and did, lose its brilliancy and power
without affecting its sway over souls already won. The
various parts were dictated, no doubt on constant re-
petition in forms not identical, and treasured up by

those who recorded them. The Prophet also, we are told, would give directions for connecting new with old, and attaching fresh revelations to the older that seemed cognate to or connected with them. It is strange, however, that he gave no more regular form to the whole body of his oracles, and left this to be done by his successors. Tradition is of no great value in determining their order, the most penetrating " higher criticism " is only partially successful, and we regretfully admit that scarcely anything quite certain has been done to solve the riddle of the Qurān.

Let us now take a few extracts from the Sacred Volume, beginning with the *Fātiha*, "Opening" Chapter, which stands out of its order at the beginning of the Qurān. To the Muslim it is much what the Paternoster is to a Roman Catholic; it is used in prayer several times a day, is held to have very special virtues, and the Prophet himself is said to have declared it to be "equal to one-third of the Qurān." Every child learns it next after the Creed, and to all for whom Arabic is a foreign tongue, as Latin is to the members of the Church of Rome, the mysterious efficacy is heightened by its unfamiliar dress, — for many decisions of the Doctors of Islām have pronounced it heresy to use in prayer translations of the Qurān, the original Arabic in which it was revealed being alone pleasing to the ears of Allāh. The prayer is used not only in religious ceremonies, but also to lend binding force to solemn agreements, at marriages, at funerals, and the like. Thus runs, in Burton's version which imitates the cadences of the original, the famous prayer, which may with advantage and instruction be

compared with the first Psalm of David and with our
own Lord's Prayer :—

"In the name of God, Merciful and Gracious !
  Praise be to Allāh, who the (three) worlds made,
  The Merciful, the Compassionate.
  The King of the Day of Faith.[1]
  Thee (alone) do we worship, and of Thee (alone) do we ask aid.
  Guide us to the Path that is straight—
  The Path of those for whom Thy Love is great, not those on
      whom is Hate, nor they that deviate.
  Amen ! O Lord of Angels, Jinns, and men !"[2]

This Chapter belongs to the early Meccan period.
  The Doctrine of Allāh—
  The Chapter of Unity (112).

> "Say, He is God alone !
> God the Eternal !
> He begets not, and is not begotten !
> Nor is there like unto Him any one !"
>   PALMER.

This the Prophet is traditionally said to have pronounced equal to one-third of the whole Qurān.

"God, there is no God but He, the living, the self-
subsisting.   Slumber takes Him not, nor sleep.   His is
what is in the heavens and what is in the earth.
Who is it that intercedes with Him, save by His permission ?   He knows what is before them and what
behind them, and they comprehend not aught of His
knowledge, but what He pleases.   His throne extends
over the heavens and the earth, and it burdens Him
not to guard them them both, for He is high and great"
(PALMER, ii. 256).

[1] Or Fate, Last Judgment (Ar. *dīn*).
[2] This line is not part of the *Fātiha* proper as it appears in the Qurān.

This is the Throne Verse, esteemed one of the grandest in the Book. Many repeat it after each of the five daily prayers, and it is often inscribed in mosques, etc. To the Jew and the Christian every phrase is familiar.

" Your God is one God; there is no God but He, the Merciful, the Compassionate. Verily, in the creation of the heavens and the earth, and the alternation of night and day, and in the ship that runneth in the sea with that which profits man, and in what water God sends down from heaven and quickens therewith the earth after its death, and spreads abroad therein all kinds of cattle, and in the shifting of the winds, and in the clouds that are pressed into service betwixt heaven and earth,—are signs to people who can understand " (PALMER, ii. 158–159).

" Say, O God, Lord of the kingdom ! Thou givest the kingdom to whomsoever Thou pleasest, and strippest the kingdom from whomsoever thou pleasest ; Thou honourest whom Thou pleasest, and abasest whom Thou pleasest ; in Thy hand is good. Verily, Thou art mighty over all. Thou dost turn night to day, and dost turn day to night, and dost bring forth the living from the dead, and dost provide for whom Thou pleasest without taking count."

" Say, If ye hide that which is in your breasts, or if ye show it, God knows it : He knows what is in the heavens and what is in the earth, for God is mighty over all."

" Say, If ye would love God, then follow me (Muhammad), and God will love you and forgive you your sins, for God is forgiving and merciful."

" Say, Obey God and the apostle ; but if ye turn

your backs, God loves not misbelievers. When He decrees a matter, He only says BE, and it is."

"God's is what is in the heavens, and what is in the earth, and unto God affairs return."

"What ye do of good surely God will not deny, for God knows those who fear."

"God is your Lord, He is the best of helpers : He is forgiving and clement. He loveth them that trust in Him. If God help you, there is none can overcome you ; but if He cast you off, who is he that can deliver you ? God is enough for us, a Good Guardian is He."

"God will not require of the soul save what it is able for. It shall have what it has earned, and it shall owe what has been earned from it. Lord, catch us not up, if we forget or go astray ; Lord, lay not on us a burden, as Thou didst upon them that were before us. Lord, make us not to bear that for which we have not strength, but forgive us, and pardon us, and have mercy on us. Thou art our King, help Thou us against the unbeliever ! "

The foregoing few extracts must suffice for textual authorities. Allāh is Almighty, All-merciful ; yet He is the Author of evil, no less than of good. Whom He will He guides aright, and whom He will He leads astray. His eternal, unchangeable, irrevocable decrees have been from all eternity inscribed on the Preserved Tablet. Yet in the beginning Islām was specially a missionary religion, to be extended over the whole world, thus sharply distinguishing it from Judaism, which rather repelled than invited converts. As we saw, however, in the Vision, Muhammad beheld Adam weeping over the myriads of his descendants who were foredoomed to hell ; another tradition tells how the

Prophet represented the Creator as fashioning His creatures and saying, as He made them, "Those for Paradise and I care not, and those for Hell and I care not!" Lane tells how at the present day in Egypt devout Muslims make no effort at the conversion of unbelievers, and justify their position by saying, "The number of the elect is fixed from everlasting, and no human acting can add to that number, or diminish aught therefrom: why should we tire ourselves with vain endeavour?" Muhammad himself was posed with the contradiction between Predestination and Freewill by his simple Arab followers in Medīna, just as in our own day Bishop Colenso was put to the worse by his "simple Zulu." But when they

> "Reasoned high
> Of Providence, fore-knowledge, will, and fate,—
> Fired fate, free-will, fore-knowledge absolute—
> And found no end, in wandering mazes lost,—"

he cut the discussion short, and declared that such disputing would bring them to hell; for "on the Judgment-day the Lord will require such as so dispute to set the matter clearly forth, and when they fail He will condemn them to hell-fire."

Of man, in his relation to God, Muhammad teaches that he is the creature of God's hand, absolutely dependent on Him for everything. From God man receives all the blessings with which he is surrounded in this life, and the promise of happiness hereafter, if he serve God and obeys Him *and His Prophet* in this life. He must pray and fast, give alms and pay tithes, go on pilgrimage to Mecca, and fight for the faith. If he die a Muslim in battle, his entry into Paradise is not

202 MUHAMMAD AND HIS POWER

only certain, but immediate : he enters at once into the
enjoyment of shady trees, cool rivers of water, wine
that rejoiceth the heart and doth not cloud the brain
and the company of black-eyed virgins of Paradise
(Hūris). This was the promise often made, though at
other times the teaching is—and such is now the
orthodox doctrine—that the dead remain in an inter-
mediate state till the general Resurrection : but believers
have all things well with them, and the wicked are
tormented with the " punishments of the grave," from
which every good Muslim prays the Lord to deliver
him. No Muslim will be condemned to hell-fire for ever,
though sin will be punished for longer or shorter time
after death, and in the end pardoned at Muhammad's
intercession.

The cardinal sins forbidden are : — Idolatry, or
associating aught with God as His equal ; adultery ;
false witness against a brother Muslim. Gaming, the
drinking of wine or any intoxicant, taking of usury,
and divination by arrows, are strictly forbidden : and
the punishment is scourging and infamy. When we
see among Christian nations all over the world the untold misery and destruction wrought by drinking and
gambling, we could wish that similar restraints were
recognised among ourselves. Yet ours is the higher
law. The Muslim is forbidden to do certain things,
and commanded to do certain others : commands and
prohibitions are alike definite and precise. The
Christian is bidden, " whether ye eat or drink, or what-
soever ye do, do all to the glory of God "; " let your
moderation be known unto all men, the Lord is at
hand " ; " love thy neighbour as thyself " ; " love worketh
no ill to his neighbour, therefore love is the fulfilling

of the law "; " be ye perfect, as your Father which is in heaven is perfect." Such is the leaven of Christianity, which shall yet leaven the whole lump of human kind: with us is the Spirit which giveth life, not the letter which killeth.   The brotherhood of Islām is limited to believers: Muslims are strictly forbidden to greet with " Peace " (*salām*) the followers of any other creed, and the one crime which must be punished by death is apostasy from Islām, as the one offence which God will not forgive is the rejection of the Prophet's message.   So strongly is the punishment of death for apostasy held to be the organic law of Islām, that the utmost efforts of the Christian powers in 1855 (when Turkey owed everything to their support) failed to get it abolished.   It must be remembered, in this connection, that Christians are, in the sight of Muslims, polytheists and idolaters, for their worship of the Son and the Holy Spirit as Persons of the Godhead: the commands of Muhammad are strict, emphatic, and often repeated, to fight to death or subjection against all such, and his own mistake may be explained by the fact that—first, the form of Christianity which he himself knew directly exalted the Virgin Mother to a level with the Father and the Son; and second, that any further knowledge he possessed was derived from Jewish sources.   We find also in the Qurān the remarkable statement, " the Jews say that Ezra is the Son of God."

Muhammad adopts the Bible's story of the creation of the world and man, his being placed in the garden of Eden, and banished therefrom for having—at the temptation of Satan—eaten of forbidden fruit, which the Arab version makes to have been wheat.   The tempter is Iblīs, who had ranked high in heaven, but who refused to obey God's command to worship Adam, as God's representative. Being condemned for his rebellion to hell-fire, he asked and obtained respite till the Judgment-day, and then swore to tempt and mislead mankind throughout the ages. Besides mankind God created the nations of the Jinns, some wicked and some good, spiritual counterparts of men. Muhammad's mission was to them also, and many believed : it is an article of faith to believe in their existence. As the ages ran, the revelation of God's will to men was made by a succession of Prophets specially commissioned with a message, gradually increasing in definiteness, until the coming of Muhammad. The earlier Prophets, of whom the first was Adam himself, and the last Jesus Christ, had a message each to his own nation only ; but the "seal of the Prophets" was to be a blessing and mercy to all mankind. The greatest of the former Prophets were Moses and Jesus Christ, but the "Father of the faithful" is (as we have seen), for Muhammad as for St. Paul, Abraham, whose Faith he was sent to revive. The other chief prophets are mainly Old Testament worthies, David, Joseph, Jonah, Elijah, and others; and those commemorated in Arab legend, Hūd, Sālih, Shuaib, whose miraculous stories are told at much length in the Qurān. The burden of every Prophet's warning is, to serve the one true God, and Him only, to know the certainty of the resurrection, and to look forward to a future life of happiness or misery, according to each man's works. The simple, beautiful histories of the Bible are amplified and distorted by a luscious and not very clean fancy, the most notable case being that of Joseph in Egypt, and it is easy to credit the tradition which tells how Muhammad wept when he found Omar reading the Jewish sacred stories; and this again lends colour to the story of the destruction of the Alexandrian libraries by that Khalifa's command, a story which Gibbon and others reject, but which De Sacy and Richard Burton believed. In the Qurān again, the births of John the Baptist and of Jesus Christ are told with many added details, and much less beauty than in the Gospels; our Lord is made Himself to deny His divinity, and the Crucifixion is branded as a profane fable. In the Traditions it is foretold that when the end of this world draws nigh, there shall arise first Dajjāl (the Muhammadan analogue of Antichrist), who shall gather to battle the hosts of evil; then Messiah shall return from heaven, to which He was caught up from the rage of the Jews, and restore the kingdom of Islām; then shall Isrāfīl blow the first blast of his trumpet, and all things that have life shall die. Death shall hold universal sway for forty days, then shall the second blast be sounded, and the dead, small and great,—animals as well as men,—shall be raised from their graves, clothed again with their bodies, and marshalled for judgment.

The great Day, ushered in by the most appalling sights and sounds, is to last for fifty thousand years! To every man will be given a book containing the record of his deeds; the righteous shall receive theirs in their right hands, and their faces will beam with joy; but the sinners will receive theirs in the left hand, chained behind their backs. Every soul will perforce confess the righteousness of the Judge. The blessed will be welcomed by the angels into Paradise, there to receive "the promise of their Lord," and for ever to enjoy rest and the reward of their faith and works,—a happiness selfish and self-centred (to say the least), not that endless life of higher service to which the Christian is taught to look forward, in the immediate presence of the Father. The wicked shall be turned into Hell, there to abide for ever in torment ever-renewed, in the "fire whose fuel is men and stones,"—filled full with unbelieving Jinns and men; and they also shall confess too late that "the promise of their Lord was true."

Some extracts from the Qurān follow, giving (generally in Palmer's version) the very words of Muhammad on the subject of man's position in this world, his duty to God and to his fellows, the final judgment and his future destiny.

"In the name of God, Merciful and Compassionate!
  When the sun is folded up,
  And when the stars do fall,
  And when the mountains are moved,
  And when the she-camels ten months gone with young shall
      be neglected,
  And when the beasts shall be crowded together,
  And when the seas shall surge up,
  And when souls shall be paired with bodies,
  And when the child who was buried alive shall ask for what
      sin she was slain,
  And when the pages shall be spread out,
  And when the heaven shall be flayed,
  And when hell shall be set ablaze,
  And when paradise shall be brought nigh,
  The soul shall know what it hath produced!" (lxxxi. 1–14).

"In the name of God, Merciful and Compassionate!
  When the heaven is cleft asunder,
  And when the stars are scattered,

And when the seas gush together,
And when the tombs are turned upside down,
The soul shall know what it hath sent on or kept back!"

"O man! what hath seduced thee concerning thy generous Lord, who created thee, and fashioned thee, and gave thee symmetry, and in what form He pleased composed thee?

"Nay, but ye call the judgment a lie! but over you are guardians set,—noble, writing down! they know what ye do!

"Verily, the righteous are in pleasure, and verily the wicked are in hell: they shall broil therein upon the Judgment-day, nor shall they be absent therefrom!

"And what shall make thee know what is the Judgment-day? Again, what shall make thee know what is the Judgment-day? a day when no soul shall control aught for another; and the bidding on that day belongs to God!" (lxxxii.).

"God it is who produced for you hearing, and sight, and intellect,—little do ye give thanks! And He it is that created you in the earth, and unto Him shall ye be gathered. And He it is who gives you life and death; and His is the alternation of life and death; have ye then no sense?

"O ye who believe! bow down and adore, and serve your Lord, and do well, haply ye may prosper; and fight strenuously for God, as is His due. He has elected you, and has not put upon you any hindrance by your religion,—the faith of your father Abraham.

"Be ye then steadfast in prayer, and give alms, and hold fast by God: He is your sovereign, and an excellent sovereign, and an excellent help.

"The servants of the Merciful are those who walk

upon the earth lowly, and when the ignorant address them say, 'Peace!' and those who pass the night adoring their Lord and standing; and those who say, 'O our Lord, turn from us the torment of hell!'

"And those who when they spend are neither wasteful nor miserly; and who call not upon another god with God, and kill not the soul which God has prohibited save deservedly; and do not commit fornication; for he who does that shall meet with a penalty; doubled shall be the torment on the Resurrection-day, and he shall therein be aye despised.

"Save he who turns again and believes, and does a righteous work; for, as to those, God will change their evil deeds to good, for God is ever forgiving, merciful!

"And those who do not testify falsely; and when they pass by vain discourse, pass it by honourably: and who are not deaf and blind when reminded of the signs of their Lord!

"Verily God leads astray whom He pleases, and guides whom He pleases!

"No burdened soul shall bear the burden of another: he who is pure is pure only for himself, and unto God the journey is.

"Those who recite the Book of God, and are steadfast in prayer, and give alms secretly and openly, hope for the merchandise that perisheth not; that He may pay them their hire, and give them increase of His grace:— verily, He is forgiving, merciful!

"He who misbelieves, his misbelief is for himself, and God knows the thoughts of men!

"Those who fear their Lord shall be driven to paradise in troops; until they come, its doors shall be opened, and its keeper shall say to them, 'Peace be upon you, ye have done well: so enter in to dwell for aye!' And they shall say, 'Praise be to God, who hath made good His promise to us! . . . And thou shalt see the angels circling round the throne, celebrating the praises of thy Lord!'

"Put not with God other gods, or thou wilt sit despised and forsaken.

"Thy Lord hath decreed that ye shall not serve other than Him! and show kindness to parents, even to old age.

"And give his due to thy kinsmen and to the traveller; and waste not wastefully, for the wasteful were ever the devil's brothers.

"Make not thy hand fettered to thy neck, neither spread it out quite open.

"And slay not your children for fear of poverty: We will provide for them.

"And draw not near to fornication: verily it is ever an abomination, and evil is the way thereof.

"And slay not the soul which God has forbidden you, save for just cause; for he that is slain unjustly, we have given his next-of-kin authority; yet let him not exceed in slaying.

"And draw not near the orphan's portion, save to increase it.

"And give full measure when ye measure out, and weigh with a right balance.

"And walk not proudly on the earth,—verily thou canst not cleave the earth, and thou shalt not reach the mountains in height."

" The fellows of the right hand,—what right lucky fellows !
   And the foremost foremost—
   These are they that are brought nigh,

14

In gardens of pleasure!
A crowd of those of yore,
And a few of those of the latter day!
And gold-weft couches, reclining on them face to face.
Around them shall go eternal youths, with goblets and ewers,
     and a cup of flowing wine; no headache shall they feel
     therefrom, nor shall their wits be dimmed!
And fruits such as they deem the best;
And flesh of fowls as they desire;
And bright and large-eyed maids like hidden pearls;
A reward for that which they have done!
They shall hear no folly and no sin;
Only the speech, 'Peace, Peace!'
And the fellows of the right—what right lucky fellows!
Amid thornless lote-trees.
And banana-trees with piles of fruit;
And outspread shade,
And water out-poured;
And fruit in abundance, neither failing nor forbidden;
And beds upraised!
Verily, we have created for them a special creation,
And made unto them virgins, darlings of equal age (with their
     spouses) for the fellows of the right!"

These and the like blessings are ever and again promised throughout the Qurān to Believers; and the wording of the promise is skilfully and tunefully varied, but the character of the delights continues always on the same low plane.

The reward is for men and women alike, as says the Book :—

"Verily—whether they be men or women—those who believe, and are devout, and truthful, and patient, and humble; who give alms, and fast, and are chaste, and remember God much,—God has prepared for them forgiveness and a great reward!" (xxxiii. 35).

Of the wicked it is said :—

"Nay, but they call the Hour a lie; but We have prepared, for those who call the Hour a lie, a blaze: when it seizes them from a far-off place, they shall hear its roaring and raging: and when they are thrown into a corner thereof, fastened together, they shall cry out to be utterly destroyed.

"And whoso rebels against God and His apostle, verily for him is the fire of hell to dwell therein for ever and ever.

"Verily, with Us are heavy fetters and hell-fire, and food that chokes and grievous woe.

"Verily, those who disbelieve in Our signs, We will broil them with fire: whenever their skins are well done, We will change them for other skins, that they may taste the torment.

"As for him who is given his book in his left hand, he shall say, 'O, would that I had not received my book! I knew not what my account would be. O, would that death had been an end of me! my wealth availed me not! my authority has perished from me!' 'Take him and fetter him, then in hell broil him! then into a chain whose length is seventy cubits force him! verily he believed not in the mighty God, nor was he careful to feed the poor: therefore he has not here to-day any warm friend, nor any food save foul ichor, which none save sinners shall eat!'"

The Qurān:—

"In the name of God, Merciful and Compassionate.

"Verily, we sent it down on the Night of Power!

"And what shall make thee know what the Night of Power is?—the Night of Power is better than a thousand months!

"The angels and the Spirit descend therein, by the permission of their Lord with every bidding.

"Peace it is until rising of the dawn!

"Verily, it is a revelation from the Lord of the worlds; the Faithful Spirit (Gabriel) came down with it upon thy heart; in plain Arabic language, . . .

"A guidance and glad tidings to the believers, who are steadfast in prayer, and give alms, and of the hereafter are sure.

"If mankind and Jinns united together to bring the like of this Qurān, they could not bring the like, though they should back each other up.

"That We might establish thy heart did We send it down piecemeal."

Muhammad :—

"Say, I am only a mortal like yourselves; I am inspired that your God is only one God. Then let him who hopes to meet his Lord do righteous deeds, and join none in the service of his Lord" (xviii. 110).

"It is a mercy from thy Lord that thou mayest warn a people to whom no warner has come before thee; haply they may take heed" (xxviii. 46).

"Will they say he has forged against God a lie? But if God pleased he could set a seal upon thy heart; but God will blot out falsehood and verify truth by His word; verily he knows the nature of men's breasts" (xlii. 25).

"Say, O ye folk! verily I am the apostle of God unto you all,—of Him whose is the kingdom of the heavens and the earth, there is no God but He! He quickens and He kills! believe then in God and His apostle,

the unlettered Prophet,—who believes in God and in
His words,—then follow Him that haply ye may be
guided" (vii. 188).

"Those who believe and do right and believe in what
is revealed to Muhammad,—and it is the truth from
their Lord,—He will cover for them their offences, and
order their hearts aright" (xlvii. 2).

"Say, I cannot control profit or harm for myself, save
what God will" (vii. 188).

The foregoing extracts amply show how great was
Muhammad's debt, for ideas, language, and imagery,
to the Hebrew Scriptures. Our limits do not permit
extracts from the long stories of the patriarchs, several
of which will be found in Lane's *Selections from the
Kurān*. These, which occur each more than once in
the Book, are clearly taken from the Jews, either from
the Old Testament or the Talmud; the Quraish taunted
Muhammad with the fact, and he defends himself in
the Qurān by vehement assertions that all his stories
were given him by direct revelation from God through
Gabriel. All this part of the Book belongs to the
"second Meccan period," and it will be remembered
that one of his warmest supporters was Khadija's
cousin, the aged and learned Jew, Waraqa. It needs,
however, no great discernment to see how inferior is
Muhammad's teaching to the great Hebrew lawgiver's:
"Hear, O Israel, the Lord our God is one Lord!" So,
too, the later code compares but ill with the Ten Words,
the "exceeding broad" law.

It has already been said how inferior to the originals
of Moses are the copies by Muhammad. One phrase
he constantly imitates: "When God would create anything, He says only BE, and *it is*," a manifest echo of

the account in Genesis of the creation of light. It will not be out of place to quote, from the story of Noah as given in the Qurān, what Sir W. Jones and other scholars after him consider the sublimest passage in the Book. It tells of the destruction of one of the patriarch's sons,—a warning to those who should reject the message of the latter-day "preacher of righteousness."

"And the ark floated on with them 'mid waves like mountains; and Noah cried to his son that had gone aside, 'O my boy! ride with us and be not with the misbelievers.' Said he, 'I will betake me to a mountain that shall save me from the water.' Said he, 'There is none to save this day from the command of God, except for him on whom He may have mercy.' And the wave came between them, and he was amongst the drowned" (xi. 44–6).

Moses and his law and his message are often quoted; and when Muhammad got to Medīna he had great hopes that the Jews would accept him as their promised Messiah; but he was soon undeceived, and was thenceforward their bitter and relentless foe. From that time the Qurān tries to do without the Hebrew Scriptures, and the law of Islām is promulgated, far inferior to that of Israel. To take but one instance, part of the plague-spot of the later system: Moses commanded that, if a woman were divorced and married to a second husband, her first husband should in no case afterwards marry her; but the law of Muhammad is, that if a husband have put away his wife by triple divorce, he may take her back again after a *true* marriage to another, who may divorce her the following day. This immoral and degrading practice is very

common.[1] Moreover, though some schools forbid them,
temporary marriages are (in Persia especially) part of
the law of Islām; and this was clearly established
by solemn decision of doctors assembled before the
Emperor Akbar.[2]

The seclusion and degradation of women in Islām
need not be dwelt on. Muhammad allows each man
four wives, and unlimited slave-concubines. The
wives may be divorced at the husband's absolute
pleasure, and the dowry regulations operate as but a
feeble restraint. The evil effects of the system have
been gravely noted by every impartial observer, and it
may be here remarked that Muhammadan writers on
ethics, such as Jalāli, advocate monogamy on moral
grounds, as strongly as a Christian writer might.
Slavery again is fully sanctioned in Islām. In his last
sermon at Mecca, when closing the Farewell Pilgrimage,
Muhammad bade his followers treat well "their wives
and their slaves"; the untold miseries of the present-
day slave-trade in Africa and in Central Asia are the
direct product of Muslim demand, and the mixed blood
throughout Arabia is one of its consequences. Censure
is checked when one reviews the history of slavery in
the Christian Roman Empire and in later Christendom;
but here again slavery is part of the system of Islām,
whereas in Europe and in America the slowly-working
leaven of Christ's doctrine, that all men are brothers in
Him, has abolished the ownership of man by man,
which is even more hurtful morally to the master than
to the slave.

[1] The interim husband is called *Mahallil*, "one who makes (the wife)
lawful." Burton is alone in preferring the form *Mustahill*.

[2] Ain i Akbari,—Blochman's *Translation*, p. 174.

CHAPTER XV

Shias and Sunnis, the Great Schism—Miracle Play of Hasan and Husain—Sūfis—Darwesh Orders—Wahhābis—Islām in Politics—Muslims in China—Conclusion.

WITH the death of Ali and the abdication of his eldest son, it might have seemed that Islām, reunited under the firm hand of Muāwiya, would continue one strong empire. More than ever did this seem assured when the principle of hereditary succession was established in the person of Yazīd. The contrary was the result: the fatal field of Karbalā, which seemed to extinguish for ever all opposition to Yazīd, sowed the seeds of the downfall of his race a few generations later, and laid the foundation of the great political schism which has done so much to weaken Islām in all succeeding ages. The beginning of the troubles goes back to the days of Uthmān, when (as we saw) a Jewish malcontent preached throughout Islām the doctrine that the headship was inalienably fixed in the Prophet's lineage, and therefore in Ali's descendants by Fātima. With the election of Ali, after the murder of his predecessor, the principle triumphed; but on his deathbed Ali himself expressly refused to ratify it: its revival in full vigour dates from the massacre of Husain and his little band. Ali had himself been harassed by the revolt of the Khārijites, a sort of "Fifth Monarchy"

sect in Islām, and it was by the hand of one of their
fanatics that he fell; and they continued for generations afterwards to be a thorn in the side of the
Khalifas. But they were never a very large party,
and their high theocratic notions were not calculated
to gather many adherents: so gradually they faded
away.

It was otherwise with the great schism of the Shias,
the partisans of the divine right of Ali, as against the
"orthodox" Sunnites, the followers (as they maintain)
of the *sunnat*, or practice, of the Prophet. The shib-
boleth of the latter, who form by far the greatest part
of Islām, is the acknowledgment of the title of Abu
Bakr, Omar, and Uthmān, as lawful Successors of the
Prophet. That title the Shias utterly deny, they heap
curses on the memories of the "Usurpers," insult their
names, tombs, and memorials, and by a strange and
perverse delusion deify the Prophet's line.

At the present day, Persia is the land of the Shia
schism, orthodox Islām follows the Sunni doctrine.
The adherents of the schism may be reckoned at
perhaps not more than ten or twelve millions, less
than one-tenth of the whole "Faithful"; but, politically,
the religious division between Persia and Turkey has
been, especially in the century that has just closed, of
vast importance, greatly weakening both as against
the overshadowing power of Russia. The Shia movement in Persia was largely national. The rallying-
point of Ali's name, as against the Syrian dynasty
which Persia both hated and feared, fell in with the
national feeling which recent Muslim conquest had
scarcely weakened. Ali had chosen Kūfa for his
capital, and the fact that its wavering and fickleness

had led to the final tragedy of his family only strengthened Persia's fervid allegiance to his claims.[1] In an
earlier chapter we have seen how legend told of the
prophetic light which beamed from generation to
generation on the brows of Muhammad's ancestors ;
with this Shia fancy connected the creation, "in the
beginning," of the "Light of Muhammad," the first
created thing, which existed for long ages — long
enough almost to satisfy a modern geologist !—before
the heavens and the earth came into being. In some
mysterious fashion the Prophet's immediate descendants
are associated with this pre-existence, and the whole
succession is semi-divine. It is easily understood how
such a doctrine brands as blasphemers, as well as
traitors, all who revolt against it. With the "orthodox"
party the succession is in the Khalifas, appointed
originally by direct vote of the "Faithful"; the Shias
hold a succession, inalienable from the Prophet's family,
of Imāms, limited to twelve, of whom the last, the
Mahdi (= "leader"), has vanished for a time from the
eyes of men, and is to return again before the end of
the world. Meanwhile, the visible headship of Islām
is in abeyance, and the faithful long for the blessed
day of his reappearance. "Imām" is a spiritual title,
meaning, in ordinary usage, the person who leads the
public prayer, and whose voice and gestures the congregation follows. In the early days of Islām, presiding
at public prayer belonged of right to the political
leader, but the Prophet's command was that the Imām
should be he who was best versed in the Qurān. The
name has been chosen by the Shias for the religious

[1] The whole subject is excellently treated in Sir L. Pelly's Introduction to the *Persian Miracle Play*.

and political chief of Islām, according to their doctrine; it is also the title used by Muhammad himself in the Traditions, when he is enforcing that passive and absolute obedience which he claimed as his own right, and which he declared was due to the Chief of the Faith. The Shias maintain, naturally, that Muhammad formally and solemnly proclaimed Ali his successor, and also that, when on his deathbed he called for a tablet and pen to write down " a direction which should keep his people from error," he intended to write down his nomination of Ali, and that Abu Bakr and Omar refused what he asked, hypocritically alleging (as they say) that the Qurān was perfect and sufficient guidance. So throughout the centuries Shia and Sunni have fought, and cursed, and slain, and enslaved one another. In Persia to this day the saying goes that " you may curse with impunity anyone and anything except the holy Imāms and the wife of the man you are addressing"; in Arabia the Persian pilgrims to Mecca are plundered and abused as heretics, and they are said to have been guilty at Medīna of the grossest and filthiest violation of the tombs of the first two Khalifas.

Once a year comes the great sacred season of the Shias, in the first ten days of Muharram, on the tenth of which month occurred the tragedy of Karbalā. During these days is performed, wherever Shias congregate, but with most pomp and ceremony in the cities of Persia, the great Miracle Play of the Martyrdom of Hasan and Husain. The house of every pious Shia who can afford it holds permanent shrines, varying in costliness according to his wealth, of the Holy Martyrs. As soon as the new moon of

Muharram is seen, the sacred ceremonies begin, though the preparation is made for a week beforehand. Shrines of the martyrs are displayed on a stage in temporary theatres, draped in black to express the mourning of every true heart; and dramatic readings are given night after night to crowded audiences of the moving tale of Husain and his little band of faithful followers hurrying through the desert to their doom before false, fickle Kūfa, whose promises had lured them to destruction. Gradually the passion of the hearers is wrought up to frenzy: sobs, and moans, and floods of tears, witness to their grief, while many even gash themselves with knives in sympathy with the old, pathetic story. On the seventh day is commemorated the wedding of Hasan's son to Husain's daughter, when the marriage rejoicings throw into heightened contrast the gloom of general massacre that follows. On the ensuing nights are told and represented the moving tale of the final conflict, with every circumstance of horror and agony: consuming thirst, unavailing valour in fight, fruitless entreaties for mercy; sword, and flame, and insult to the dead,—all is faithfully and minutely depicted. So real are the passions excited that Yazīd's men are pelted and cursed, and it has even happened that the "murderer of Husain" has himself been murdered by a frenzied fanatic. With the tenth day the ceremonies end, the empty shrines being cast into the water,—and the final prayers are said. The whole ceremonies are vivid and impressive, and the annual celebration keeps strongly alive the great schism of Islām: in Bombay, and elsewhere in India, it often needs the strong hand of military power to prevent riot and bloodshed between the rival sects.

The tenth of Muharram, it may be noted, is observed
by Sunnis as a great and most excellent day, that
on which the Almighty created Adam and Eve, His
throne, the pen, the Tablet of fate, life and death,
Heaven and Hell.

Into the Miracle Play are introduced scenes in
heaven, Muhammad, and Ali, and Fātima; and the
doctrine of prevailing intercession with the Almighty
is carried to an extreme, teaching which is directly
opposed to that of the Prophet himself.

As the Shia heresy rests on the cult of Ali as semi-
divine, so are traced back to him also the singular
doctrines of Sūfiism, which also is the corruption of
Islām by the mysticism of Persia and perhaps also
the pantheism of India. The cardinal doctrine of
Muhammad is that the Creator is absolutely exalted
above the creation, which came into existence by the
word of His power, and that the individual souls of
His creatures will after death be judged by Him and
receive from Him their doom for eternity. The very
opposite of this is the Sūfi teaching. It came into
prominence about two centuries after the Flight, and
gave for about one hundred and fifty years a dynasty
to Persia, the memory of which survives in our own
tongue in the word "Sophy" for the king of Persia.
To-day its countless schools of Faqirs or Darweshes
(Arabic and Persian respectively for "Mendicant") are
spread through the whole domain of Islām, and in
their various orgiastic rites as "howling," "dancing,"
"whirling," and the like, present to the foreigner
the most striking caricature of their religion. No
saying of Muhammad was more characteristic than
this: "There is no monkery in Islām," and withdrawal

from the active duties of civil and social life he constantly and severely censured. Moreover, it is fundamental that every man makes approach for himself to the Creator : there is no regular established priesthood, but any Muslim is qualified to lead public devotions. All this we shall find ignored or reversed in the mystical system of the Sūfis, whose votaries are to be found in every corner of Islām.

The origin of the name, as of so many religious terms, is disputed. Some connect it with the Arabic *sāf*, "pure," because purity of heart is the first requisite; others with *sūf*, "wool," because the votary's dress is of coarse woollen stuff; but more probably the name is originally the Greek σοφία, that transcendental wisdom to which the Gnostics aspired and pretended. The same passion which drove the early Christians in thousands to solitude in the deserts of Arabia and Egypt, which in all ages since has sent others crowding into monasteries, drove Muslim devotees—hungering after a more spiritual doctrine than the formal religion of the Founder, to group themselves in communities round teachers of special repute for sanctity. To the head of his community, the *Pîr* ("Ancient") or *Murshid* ("Director"), the most absolute obedience was paid; the ceremonies of initiation vary, and the degrees of austerity required are at the absolute discretion of the head; the special teaching given is secret, and the disciples are discouraged or even prohibited from revealing it. But the main doctrine is the same throughout. The soul of man is in exile, imprisoned in the body; it is an emanation from God, and—by a gloss on Muhammad's doctrine, "To Him do we return,"—the Sūfis teach that the ultimate aim of man is to win reunion with or absorption in the Divine. To attain to this is his end, and the means are detachment from the world, its pleasures and its pains, self-discipline, unwearied meditation on God, absolute devotion to Him. The pathway to perfection is the Sūfi's pilgrimage; the soul is one with the Creator, and when at last that Oneness is realised, the Union is complete, and the soul finds its perfect bliss, losing itself and its personal consciousness in Him, a state which it is not easy to distinguish from the Buddhist Nirvāna. In regard to religion, the Sūfis hold that only in the lowest stage of the quest after perfection are external observances binding on or serviceable to the devout soul. As soon as the disciple is fully penetrated with love to God, he becomes "free from the law"; Divine love driving out from his heart all worldly desires, he reaches the stage of "seclusion," Zuhd; occupying himself then with exclusive meditation on the nature and perfections of God, he attains to "knowledge"; "knowledge" carries him forward to "ecstasy," in which he receives a revelation of the true nature of Godhead, the stage of "truth"; from this he advances to the last stage, "union" with the Divine,—which may be reached even in this life, though the final consummation, "absorption," does not take place till the "muddy vesture of decay" is put off.

Such is the Sūfis' mystical journey, and it is easy to see how dangerous to morality is a system which at an early stage casts off all the outward restraints of religion. With a mixture of fatalism, sanctioned by the words of the Qurān, they hold that all men's actions are really controlled and foreordained, and therefore that man is not morally responsible for his deeds. Nay, the devotee who deems himself to have attained to "union" has been heard to proclaim himself God, and to suffer death for the blasphemy. The highest expression of these Shia doctrines, the Bible (so to speak) of the sect, is contained in the mystical poetry of Persia,—in Jāmī, Hāfiz, Jalāl ud din, and others; there Wine and Love are the emblems of spiritual aspirations—and the imagery is carried to extreme lengths.

The Sūfis are divided into many sects and schools, but we need not pursue the subject. Nor need we notice other divisions and heresies of Islām that have during the ages developed; the eternal problem of Fate and Free-will, the controversies on the Being and attributes of God, and the other religious questions raised or stimulated by contact with other races and systems of thought. But the strange revival of orthodox doctrine and practice, the creed of the Wahhābis, must be briefly noticed, especially as at one time it bade fair to have important political results.

It was founded in the early part of the eighteenth century, and was an attempt to restore Islām to its earliest purity, freed from the corruptions which had defaced it from the grand simplicity of its Founder and his contemporaries. Championed by some able and ambitious chiefs of Najd, a dynasty was founded and still rules in Central Arabia, though much shorn of the power which once it wielded. Burkhardt and Palgrave specially studied the revival, and the latter has written on the subject a most charming and learned book. He found that in the capital of Muslim orthodoxy, nearly forty years ago, formalism and bigotry reigned supreme, but the moral law was reduced to the avoidance of polytheism and abstinence from wine and tobacco! All other crimes and offences were venial: "Allāh is very Pitiful,"—but idolatry and "drinking the shameful," that is smoking, should find forgiveness neither in this world nor the next. Wahhābi tenets spread widely among the Mussulmans of India, and at one time assumed a threatening aspect; but the danger is now at all events latent. But the horrors of the great Mutiny, and the constant troubles from fanatics on the northern and western frontiers of the peninsula, with the events of recent years from the pretended Mahdi and his Khalifa in the Soudān, warn us what terrible forces are still at the call of Islām.

In India there has been an interchange of evil between Islām and Hinduism: the former has adopted much of the spirit of caste and the idolatrous worship of saints and sacred shrines, and has given in exchange the ruinous system of the seclusion of women,—so easy is the infection of evil! Among the most important conquests of the Prophet's faith, however, are some of the fairest and richest provinces of China, and they may yet play a great part in the history of the Far East. The attempt, twenty-five years ago, to found a strong power in Central Asia failed; Yarkand was crushed between Russia and China, as between the upper and nether millstones; but since that time the Mussulmans of China, some of the best, most warlike, and most enterprising material to be found in the empire, are said to have increased from an estimated twenty millions to thirty millions; and the shrewd

German Emperor suggested but the other day to his "friend and ally" at Constantinople that a Holy War should be preached among them against the Manchu tyranny. That such a movement is possible no one will deny, though it is strange to find the project championed by a Christian monarch, who perhaps dreams of reviving in Europe the Holy Roman Empire!

In the foregoing pages I have attempted briefly to tell the history of the rise and early conquests of one of the great religions of the world, and especially to tell the life-story of its Founder. Sprung from one of the noblest families of Mecca, the immemorial shrine of idol-worship for all Arabia, he grew up amidst idolatry; but in early manhood he caught the breeze of revolt from that gross superstition in which he had been nurtured, and for many years stood forth among his people to witness for and preach a purer faith,—the mark of scorn, insult, and persecution. Gradually his genius, earnestness, and high moral character gathered round him a little band of followers, men and women of all ranks, and all alike absolutely devoted to their leader. When the fit time came, when he was assured of a welcome and power in Medina, he forsook his native city; slowly and cautiously, but never wavering in his ambitious plans, he won his way into the hearts of men and built up a strong power in Arabia, bound together by faith in his mission, and that absolute devotion to his person which only the rarest of men can command. But as his power grew, his character suffered. The lust of rule ate like a canker into his soul; he shrank from no cruelty or treachery to compass his ends, though he was never cruel when unreserved

submission was made.   His debt to the Jews and to
their Scriptures may be read in every page of his Book,
yet he shrank not from the blasphemy of saying that
every word of his pretended revelation had been given
to him directly by God through the Archangel Gabriel.
He justified his vagrant love and his jealousy of his
wives by the command of the Almighty, registered (as
he taught) from all eternity in the highest heaven.
Shutting his eyes to the purer light of Jewish and
Christian revelation, he assumed by his own teaching
to supersede them both.   Yet we have seen that the
morality of the latest, falls far below that of the earlier
religions; the whole position of women was changed for
the worse, and instead of the equal and help of her husband the wife was degraded to be his slave and his toy;
slavery was sanctioned as of divine institution for all
time; the savage law of retaliation and blood-revenge
was re-enacted, and the inhuman and barbarous penal-
ties of mutilation for theft and robbery were commanded.   Freedom of thought and liberty of conscience
were stifled, and the sword was called in to compel when
persuasion failed.   When he meddled with the calendar,
Muhammad made inextricable confusion.   Presumptuously declaring that on a certain day the seasons had
returned to the point at which they stood when God
placed man upon earth, he fixed a lunar year of twelve
months, which has been ever since a source of trouble
and annoyance.   Professing to establish a universal
religion, he stultified himself by laying down rules for
the annual month of fasting which could by no possi-
bility be observed in extreme northern or extreme
southern latitudes.   Tried, in fact, by all those tests
which he himself challenged, his religion is shown to be

not of God and himself to lie under the condemnation he pronounces on those who speak without warrant in God's name.

I have briefly outlined the early political conquests of the new faith, when under able captains the resistless valour of Arabia's locust-like swarms of warriors subdued the fairest and most fruitful lands of Asia and northern Africa, strongholds which it possesses to this day. We have seen how soon wealth corrupted the first simplicity of Islâm, how ambition deluged its kingdoms with civil bloodshed, and yet how firm a grasp that false system still has over one-sixth of the whole human race ; and how deeply founded is, after nearly thirteen hundred years, the baleful power of Muhammad.

If it be thought that the judgment passed on the Prophet of Arabia is harsh, let it be remembered that the evidence on which it rests comes all from the lips and the pens of his own devoted adherents. The voice of foes or detractors of his own time, or of time immediately following, has not reached the ears of later ages. Everything that could tend to his glory was eagerly sought out and treasured up by men jealous of his good name, and everything that might seem to detract therefrom was carefully suppressed. His lightest words were sacred to them, his most trifling actions were the example they strove to follow. To them he was highest and most excellent of the creatures of God's hand, last and most perfect of the messengers who declared His will to man. The vast body of tradition which was traced back to the lips of those who had most closely companied with him was jealously sifted and scrutinised, though not tested by the canons of

western criticism; it is on this that our knowledge
is founded, and our judgment passed, — and the
followers of the Prophet can scarcely complain if,
even on such evidence, the verdict of history goes
against him.

APPENDICES

APPENDIX A.

Woman and the Future Life.

Muhammad taught clearly and definitely (Q. xxxiii. 35) that Paradise was to be the reward of good women no less than of good men. He left, however, the nature of their enjoyments to be inferred. But the not uncommon belief that Muslims hold that women either have no souls, or that their souls perish at the death of the body, is no groundless calumny of the Christian. If Hood sang of

> " the barbarous Turk,
> Where woman has never a soul to save,"

the Prophet himself said that " Hell was for the most part peopled with women "; and there is remarkable recent evidence that the belief that women do *not* live after death is held by educated Muslims.

Sir Edward Malet, in his charming book of recollections (*Shifting Scenes*), records a conversation he had with the late Khedive of Egypt (Taufiq), Tewfik Pasha, for whom Sir Edward had high regard. There was fear that the rebels would storm the palace and murder the Khedive and all his

family, and Tewfik explained the abject terror of his wives by
saying, "For them, you know, existence ends absolutely with
death." If the Khedive of Egypt held such a belief, it is
probably common among his co-religionists.

APPENDIX B.

The Mussulman Calendar.

The Muhammadan Era (A.H.) dates from the Flight of the
Prophet from Mecca to Medīna, A.D. 622. It begins, however,
not from the day of the Flight, but from 1st Muharram of that
(Arab) year, corresponding to April–May. The old Arab
year, like the Greek, was luni-solar, a correction being made
by intercalary months as required : the system, according to
Al Bīrūnī, was borrowed from the Jews. But at the Farewell
Pilgrimage, in the last year of his life, Muhammad by proclamation (Q. ix. 38) abolished the intercalary system as a
pagan usage, and declared that thenceforward the years should
consist each of twelve lunar months. The Hijra Era was
officially instituted by Omar, seventeen years after the Flight.

The present year 1901 A.D. is 1319 A.H. (20th April =
1 Muharram), and the complex rule for converting the year
A.H. into A.D. is as follows (H. H. Wilson): Multiply the
H. year by 2977, the difference between 100 solar and 100
Muhammadan years : divide the product by 100, and
deduct the quotient from the A.H. ; then add to the result
621·569,—and the sum is the A.D. The rule for the conversion of A.D. into A.H. is even more complicated.

The old Arab names for the months of the year were

retained in Islām, and had been given from the natural character of the seasons. When, therefore, owing to the lunar computation, the months gradually retrograded through the whole year, the names were often absurdly at variance with the reality of the season. One effect of the change has been to make the severity of the Fast of Ramadhān to vary from year to year.

APPENDIX C.

An Original Despatch of Muhammad.

Sir W. Muir expresses in his *Life of Mahomet* a hope, which is not unreasonable, that we may yet recover the original letters of protection granted by the Prophet to Christian chiefs. We do, however, possess the equally interesting summons addressed, in 7 A.H., to Muqauqas, Governor of Egypt, calling upon him to embrace Islām. An identical summons was addressed (see pp. 121 and foll.) to the Emperor Heraclius, the King of Persia, and others.

The despatch already existed in the Traditions, as having been handed down by Ibn Abbās, who cites that which was addressed to Heraclius. The original document, which the late learned Dr. P. Badger declared to be genuine, was discovered in 1858 by some French travellers at a convent in Upper Egypt, and is now preserved at Constantinople. It is thus translated by Dr. Badger :

"In the Name of God, the Pitiful, the Compassionate! From Muhammad, the servant of God and His Prophet, to Mukaukis, the head of the Copts. Peace be upon him who follows the right way (Islām). Further, I write you to embrace Islām : become a Muslim and you will be saved, (and) God will vouchsafe you a double reward ; but if you decline, you will be answerable for the calamities which shall befall the Copts. [1] *O, people of the Book* (having Sacred Scriptures), *come ye to a just judgment between us and you.—That we worship not aught but God, and that we associate nothing with Him* (as a plurality of persons), *and that the one of us take not the other for lords* (Rabbis) *beside God. Then if they decline, say : Bear ye witness that we are Muslims.*"

(*Seal*)

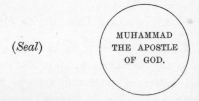

MUHAMMAD
THE APOSTLE
OF GOD.

The above is taken from Sir. W. Smith's *Dictionary of Christian Biography*, art. MUHAMMAD (by Dr. G. Badger).

[1] Qurān iii. 57.

INDEX

THE WORLD'S EPOCH-MAKERS.

A Series of Biographical Studies dealing with Prominent Epochs in Theology, Philosophy, and the History of Intellectual Development.

EDITED BY OLIPHANT SMEATON.

Each Volume contains on an average 250 pages, and is published at 3s. The Volumes will *not* appear in strict chronological sequence.

I. BUDDHA AND BUDDHISM. The First Bursting of the Fetters of Ignorance and Superstition. By ARTHUR LILLIE, M.A., London.
[*Now ready.*

II. SOCRATES. The Moral Awakening of the Western World. By Rev. J. T. FORBES, M.A., Edinburgh. [*Shortly.*

III. PLATO. By Professor D. G. RITCHIE, M.A., University of St. Andrews.

IV. MARCUS AURELIUS AND THE LATER STOICS. The Last and the Greatest Age of Stoicism. By F. W. BUSSELL, D.D., Vice-Principal of Brasenose College, Oxford. [*Shortly.*

V. ORIGEN AND GREEK PATRISTIC THEOLOGY. By Rev. W. FAIRWEATHER, M.A. [*Now ready.*

VI. AUGUSTINE AND LATIN PATRISTIC THEOLOGY. By Rev. Professor B. B. WARFIELD, D.D., Princeton.

VII. MUHAMMAD AND HIS POWER. By P. DE LACY JOHNSTONE, M.A.(Oxon.). [*Now ready.*

VIII. ANSELM AND *CUR DEUS HOMO*. By Rev. A. C. WELCH, B.D.
[*Now ready.*

IX. FRANCIS AND DOMINIC AND THE MENDICANT ORDERS. By Rev. Professor J. HERKLESS, D.D., University of St. Andrews.
[*Now ready.*

X. SCOTUS ERIGENA AND HIS EPOCH. By R. LATTA, Ph.D., D.Sc., Professor of Moral Philosophy in the University of Aberdeen.

XI. WYCLIF AND THE LOLLARDS. By Rev. J. C. CARRICK, B.D.

XII. THE MEDICI AND THE ITALIAN RENAISSANCE. By OLIPHANT SMEATON, M.A., Edinburgh.

[*Continued on next page.*

THE WORLD'S EPOCH-MAKERS—*continued.*

XIII. THE TWO BACONS AND EXPERIMENTAL SCIENCE. Showing how ROGER BACON prepared the way for FRANCIS BACON LORD VERULAM. By Rev. W. J. COUPER, M.A.

XIV. SAVONAROLA. By Rev. G. M'HARDY, D.D. [*Now ready.*

XV. LUTHER AND THE GERMAN REFORMATION. By Rev. Professor T. M. LINDSAY, D.D., U.F.C. College, Glasgow.
[*Now ready.*

XVI. CRANMER AND THE ENGLISH REFORMATION. By A. D. INNES, M.A.(Oxon.), London. [*Now ready.*

XVII. CALVIN AND THE REFORMED THEOLOGY. By Rev. Principal SALMOND, D.D., U.F.C. College, Aberdeen.

XVIII. PASCAL AND THE PORT ROYALISTS. By Professor W. CLARK, LL.D., D.C.L., Trinity College, Toronto.

XIX. DESCARTES, SPINOZA, AND THE NEW PHILOSOPHY. By Rev. Professor J. IVERACH, D.D., U.F.C. College, Aberdeen.

XX. WILLIAM HERSCHEL AND HIS WORK. By JAMES SIME, M.A., F.R.S.E. [*Now ready.*

XXI. WESLEY AND METHODISM. By F. J. SNELL, M.A.(Oxon.).
[*Now ready.*

XXII. LESSING AND THE NEW HUMANISM. Including Baumgarten and the Science of Æsthetics. By Rev. A. P. DAVIDSON, M.A.

XXIII. HUME AND HIS INFLUENCE ON PHILOSOPHY AND THEOLOGY. By Professor J. ORR, D.D., Glasgow.

XXIV. ROUSSEAU AND NATURALISM IN LIFE AND THOUGHT. By Professor W. H. HUDSON, M.A., Leland Stanford Junior University, California.

XXV. KANT AND HIS PHILOSOPHICAL REVOLUTION. By Professor R. M. WENLEY, D.Sc., Ph.D., University of Michigan.

XXVI. SCHLEIERMACHER AND THE REJUVENESCENCE OF THEOLOGY. By Professor A. MARTIN, D.D., New College, Edinburgh. [*Shortly.*

XXVII. HEGEL AND HEGELIANISM. By Professor R. MACKINTOSH, D.D., Lancashire Independent College, Manchester.

XXVIII. NEWMAN AND HIS INFLUENCE. By C. SAROLEA, Ph.D., Litt. Doc., University of Edinburgh.

HOW TO READ THE PROPHETS:

Being the Prophecies arranged Chronologically in their Historical Setting, with Explanations, Maps, and Glossary.

BY REV. BUCHANAN BLAKE, B.D.

Now Complete, in Five Volumes Crown 8vo.

Part I. THE PRE-EXILIAN MINOR PROPHETS (with JOEL). *Second Edition.* Price 4s.

Part II. ISAIAH (Chapters i.-xxxix.). *Second Edition.* Price 2s. 6d.

Part III. JEREMIAH. Price 4s.

Part IV. EZEKIEL. Price 4s.

Part V. ISAIAH (xl.-lxvi.) and THE POST-EXILIAN PROPHETS. Price 4s.

N.B.—The Series being now complete, Messrs. Clark offer the SET of FIVE VOLUMES for FIFTEEN SHILLINGS.

"*It has often been found a difficulty to profit fully from the reading, especially of the smaller prophecies of the Old Testament. To make these prophecies intelligible to the plainest reader, it seems desirable that a chronological arrangement of the prophetic books should be attempted. Alongside of the several prophecies should be placed those portions of the Old Testament historical books which deal with the same period. The aim of these manuals is consequently in this direction: to bring within the reach of the many a clear and succinct presentation of these prophets in their historical environment.*"—From the AUTHOR'S INTRODUCTION.

"Those who already possess the earlier parts of the same work will at once possess themselves of this new volume. Those who do not, will be glad to have it recommended to their notice. The author's plan has grown since he first announced it, and we are glad of it, as the treatment is more full and thorough. It is enough now to say that there is nothing like this little book on Jeremiah."—*Church Bells.*

"Mr Blake has already taught us how to read Isaiah and the Minor Prophets, and we have found the task much lightened in consequence, scarcely any more a toilsome task at all. For the difficulty of the Prophets is in their arrangement, together with the numerous allusions, local and historical, and these are the things Mr Blake takes pains to put right for us. He puts them right, so that now we stand, as far as it is possible we ever could stand, in the same position as the prophet's hearers. No 'Aids to the Study of the Bible' can approach these in real helpfulness for the ordinary Bible reader."—*The Expository Times.*

"A pleasure to read, and profit for the reading. . . . The arrangement of the historical sections, and the prophetical utterances connected therewith, is admirable. All Bible students have reason to be grateful to the author for this entertaining volume; its form is inviting, its interest absorbing."—*Church Times.*

"A well-conceived and carefully executed attempt to make these writings speak for themselves. . . . His book will give a new meaning to these prophecies to many a reader."—*The Critical Review.*

EDINBURGH: T. & T. CLARK, 38 GEORGE STREET.
LONDON: SIMPKIN, MARSHALL, HAMILTON, KENT & CO., LTD.

BY PROFESSOR W. N. CLARKE, D.D.

The *Bookman* says : 'Dr. Clarke's charm both of thought and expression secures a welcome for anything he may write.'

1. AN OUTLINE OF CHRISTIAN THEOLOGY.

Seventh Edition now ready, post 8vo, price 7s. 6d.

'It is difficult to speak of this book in adequate terms without an appearance of exaggerated praise. . . . Here at last the great vital truths of the Christian faith are set along the lines of the highest thought of the liberal, reverent, modern mind, and with consummate skill and fascinating interest. Theology is no doubt the queen of the sciences, but, as usually presented, in somewhat austere, ponderous, antiquated guise, has little human attraction. Here it is quick with human interest, answering to the living thoughts of the living generation.'—*Puritan.*

2. WHAT SHALL WE THINK OF CHRISTIANITY?

Crown 8vo, price 2s. 6d.

'Dr. Clarke's "Outline of Christian Theology" had a reception rarely accorded to an American book, and the sale is briskly proceeding. The new little book is written in the same charming simplicity of language, and its thoughts are as great and simple, that it is likely to find an equally warm welcome beside its elder brother. There are three chapters: (1) The Christian People; (2) The Christian Doctrine; (3) The Christian Power.'—*Expository Times.*

3. CAN I BELIEVE IN GOD THE FATHER?

Just published, crown 8vo, price 3s.

'Dr. Clarke has here, as elsewhere, shown himself a master in the arts of popularising Christian apologetics.'—*Christian World.*

ST. PAUL'S CONCEPTION OF CHRIST;

or, The Doctrine of the Second Adam. Being the Sixteenth Series of the 'Cunningham Lectures.' By DAVID SOMERVILLE, D.D. In demy 8vo, price 9s.

'By its keen and profound insight, by its sanity, and by its fulness of knowledge, the volume will at once take its place as the best authority on that department of New Testament theology with which it deals.'—*Critical Review.*

THE CHRIST OF HISTORY AND OF EXPERIENCE.

Being the 'Kerr Lectures' for 1897. By DAVID W. FORREST, D.D. In post 8vo, Third and Revised Edition, price 6s.

'An exceedingly able treatment of a great and important subject.'—The late Professor CALDERWOOD.

BIBLE CLASS PRIMERS.

EDITED BY REV. PRINCIPAL SALMOND, D.D.

In paper covers, 6d. each; free by post, 7d. In cloth, 8d. each; free by post, 9d.

The History of the English Bible, and How It has come down to Us. By Rev. W. BURNET THOMSON, M.A., B.D. With Illustrations of MSS.

Historical Geography of the Holy Land. With 42 Illustrations. By Rev. S. R. MACPHAIL, D.D.

Our Lord's Illustrations. By Rev. R. RESKER, M.A.

Elijah and Elisha. By Rev. R. G. MACINTYRE, B.D.

The Exile and the Restoration. By Professor A. B. DAVIDSON, D.D.

The Miracles of Our Lord. By Professor J. LAIDLAW, D.D.

Christian Conduct; Christian Character: A Study in New Testament Morality. By Professor T. B. KILPATRICK, D.D.

The Free Church of Scotland. By Rev. C. G. M'CRIE, D.D.

The Making of Israel. By Rev. C. A. SCOTT, B.D.

The Truth of Christianity. By Rev. Professor IVERACH, D.D.

The Sabbath. By Rev. Principal SALMOND, D.D.

Our Christian Passover. By Rev. C. A. SALMOND, M.A.

The Kingdom of God. A Plan of Study. In Three Parts. By Rev. F. HERBERT STEAD, M.A. (Or the Three Parts in one vol., cloth, 1s. 6d.)

The Parables of Our Lord. By Rev. Principal SALMOND, D.D.

Life of St. John. By PATON J. GLOAG, D.D.

Life of Abraham. By Rev. C. A. SCOTT, B.D.

Historical Connection between the Old and New Testaments. By Rev. Professor JOHN SKINNER, M.A., D.D.

The Life of Christ. By Rev. Principal SALMOND, D.D.

The Shorter Catechism. In Three Parts. By Rev. Principal SALMOND, D.D. (Or in one vol., cloth, 1s. 6d.)

The Period of the Judges. By the Rev. Professor PATERSON, D.D.

Outlines of Protestant Missions. By JOHN ROBSON, D.D.

Life of the Apostle Peter. By Rev. Principal SALMOND, D.D.

Outlines of Early Church History, By the late Rev. HENRY WALLIS SMITH, D.D.

Life of David. By the late Rev. PETER THOMSON, M.A.

Life of Moses. By Rev. Professor IVERACH, D.D.

'Accurately done, clear, mature, and scholarly.'—*Christian.*

Life of Paul. By PATON J. GLOAG, D.D.

'This little book could not well be surpassed.'—*Daily Review.*

Life and Reign of Solomon. By Rev. RAYNER WINTERBOTHAM, M.A., LL.B.

'Every teacher should have it.'—Rev. C. H. SPURGEON.

The History of the Reformation. By Rev. Professor WITHEROW.

'A vast amount of information set forth in a clear and concise manner.'—*United Presbyterian Magazine.*

The Kings of Israel. By Rev. W. WALKER, M.A.

'A masterpiece of lucid condensation.'—*Christian Leader.*

The Kings of Judah. By Rev. Professor GIVEN, Ph.D.

'Admirably arranged; the style is sufficiently simple and clear to be quite within the compass of young people.'—*British Messenger.*

Joshua and the Conquest. By Rev. Professor CROSKERY.

'This carefully written manual will be much appreciated.'—*Daily Review.*

Bible Words and Phrases. Explained and Illustrated. By Rev. CHARLES MICHIE, M.A. 18mo, cloth, 1s.

'Will be found interesting and instructive, and of the greatest value to young students and teachers.'—*Athenæum.*

The Seven Churches of Asia. By DEBORAH ALCOCK. 18mo, cloth, 1s.